THE ADVENTUROUS BOY'S HANDBOOK

THE ADVENTUROUS BOY'S HANDBOOK

Edited by
Stephen Brennan and Finn Brennan

Skyhorse Publishing

With much love,

to Jennifer and to Lara,

the adventurous girls in our family.

Skyhorse Publishing books may be purchased in bulk at special discounts for sales promotion, corporate gifts, fund raising, or educational purposes. Special editions can also be created to specifications. For details, contact Special Sales Department, Skyhorse Publishing, 555 Eighth Avenue, Suite 903, New York, NY 10018 or info@skyhorsepublishing.com.

www.skyhorsepublishing.com

10 9 8 7 6 5 4 3 2 1

Library of Congress Cataloging-in-Publication Data

Brennan, Stephan.
   The adventurous boy's handbook / by Stephan Brennan and Finn Brennan.
      p. cm.
   Includes index.
   ISBN-13: 978-1-60239-222-9 (alk. paper)
   ISBN-10: 1-60239-222-6 (alk. paper)
   1. Outdoor life--Juvenile literature. I. Brennan, Finn. II. Title.
   GV191.62.B73 2008
   796.5--dc22

                              2008004308

Printed in China

ACKNOWLEDGMENTS

Many thanks to Tony Lyons and Bill Wolfsthal at Skyhorse Publishing for seeing the possibilities of this book. Also to Ann Treistman, our superb editor, for first suggesting that Finn and I do this together, and for all her guidance and leadership.

Many thanks also to James Langlois for helping to assemble this book.

CONTENTS

DEFENSIVE FIGHTING SKILLS

CLASSIC BASEBALL

MORE THINGS THE ADVENTUROUS BOY
SHOULD KNOW

THE ADVENTUROUS BOY'S HANDBOOK

INTRODUCTION

"My childhood bends beside me."
— *Ulysses*

What a splendid idea it was to do this book with my son. Not only has it allowed Finn and me the once-in-a-lifetime opportunity to structure our time together to some tangible purpose, but also it permits us to experience the historically complex but important relationship between man and boy. And on the purely practical level, each of us has both stimulated and checked the other's interests and excesses. Indeed, the other day I was chatting with my co-author, bantering really—you know, the usual thing, and I asked him to tell me what *adventure* was—to describe it. He cocked his head and looked at me as though I must have lost my mind. Why, he surely wondered, after all the work assembling this book, after all the hikes, expeditions and forays in the wilderness, after all the trips to the library, the hours on the Internet, the discussions and disagreements, was his father putting this obvious question to him? Then looking off into the middle distance, he said very simply:

"Adventure is when you go into the woods and stay there a real long time—so long that Mom begins to get worried—doing things. It's tracking a deer or a rabbit in the snow. It's looking to discover a fossil that no one has ever seen before. It's seeing how close you can get to a flock of wild turkeys without them running away. It's swimming in a new place, or going fishing with Grampa. Any boat ride is an adventure. It's finding a perfect stick, and pretending it's a gun or maybe even a magic sword."

"What about books?" I asked, "Can reading itself be an adventure?"

"It can be," he said, "if the story is exciting, and full of troubles and dangers; and if the good guys win."

"What about reading something that's not a story? What about all the how-to stuff we have in our book? Is that adventure?"

"It is if it's something you can use in an adventure, or if it lets you imagine a real-life adventure, then it is."

"How about a book that teaches, say . . . about the different birds?"

"Are there pictures?" he asks.

"Yes, well some . . ."

"Pictures are good," he says as he sits and flips the pages of the manuscript. "I like the stuff about life-saving."

Finn, and any young boy of a curious mind, appreciates the merits of an extensive training in the arts of camping, archery, hunting, fishing and orienteering—for a young boy needs to learn these skills to embark on his own adventures, be they grounded in reality or in the realms of imagination. This book focuses on the practical skills that boys in this generation perhaps know less of than their fathers. The ability to tie useful knots, treat a snake bite, survive in the wilderness and read approaching clouds during the day and stars at night, are all skills that a courageous and inquisitive boy will need to craft his own adventures.

It really does appear that all men are boys right from the start; and that a man remains a boy on some level straight on through his life. Boys will be boys, so say all the experts. Depending on one thing and another, this may be seen as a good or bad thing. And anyone who has ever parented a boy—or married a man—will tell you this is so. For our purposes then, we grant this holy state or kingdom of boyhood, recognizing that a boy may be of any age. We are quite willing to take the bad with the good, and we ignore the esoteric questions of whether these qualities are due to nature or to nurture. Our aim is to construct a handbook of subjects that may be said to be of special interest to boys.

(A word about that: These days, anyone with half a brain agrees that rock-climbing, fishing, swimming, fossil-hunting, self-defense, and every topic in this book will be of just as great an interest to girls as it is to boys. Adventure is adventure, after all, and every one of us falls under its spell at one time or another. We're not disputing any of this. It may well be that to do a boy's book means accepting this vast cliché. We do it with open eyes, knowing full well that it may cause some of the girls and women in our lives to pause. "Read it," implores Finn, "You'll love it, whether you're a boy or not.")

The closing decades of the nineteenth century, with the industrialization of printing, began what we must consider to be a half-century-long golden age of "boy's" books. Many of our greatest authors, like Twain and Kipling, Crane and Stevenson, wrote tales for boys. In Britain, Alfred George Henty pioneered the historical novel for boys with books like *Under Drake's Flag* and *With Clive in India*. In the 1890s the German author, Karl May, wrote the boy's adventure classics *In the Desert* and the three volume *Winnetou* saga. Whole syndicates sprang up, devoted to feeding the market for the stories of Horatio Alger, Tom Swift and the Hardy Boys. The non-fiction books of how-to and other volumes of advice for young men were also hugely popular and potent works.

There's something about this flowering of the genre that is still mightily attractive, and so for our book we've consciously chosen to reflect these traditions by excerpting works from some of the masters: Daniel C. Beard on odd modes of fishing, or Charles Ledyard Norton on the rigging and sailing of small boats, for instance. The work of Ernest Thompson Seton, who helped found the Boy Scouts of America, was also an important resource. Few writers are as good as he is on all the various aspects of woodsmanship. There is also a section by Fay E. Ward on cowboying which is just perfect for our guide. Not all our contributors are graybeards. Some of our chapters are excerpted largely from the *U. S. Army Field Manual* and the *U. S. Army Ranger Handbook*. Other information has been gleaned from sporting manuals and the Internet. In rendering this material we've tried wherever possible for an easy, off-handed, avuncular approach, that fully respects the information we want to get across, but does so in a voice that maximizes its accessibility.

As Finn and I work together, looking at the worn and tattered pages of books I read as a boy, my hand rests on his shoulder. He asks if we can go fishing after lunch. I nod, a lump in my throat.

Stephen Brennan
Finn Brennan
March 2008

CAMPING

PITCHING A TENT

A tent will be a great addition to the comfort of your camp. If you have a piece of awning, canvas, old sail or plastic sheet you may improvise a tent. It can be thrown over the clothesline, or a clothesline prop may be used, supported at each end by forked sticks, and the canvas pegged down at the sides. In case there are no eyelets with which to attach tent-ropes and you do not wish to injure the material, the sides may be secured by allowing them to rest upon a plank and fastening them there with a strip of wood nailed over the canvas. The nails in this case are driven in at the ends of the strip only, and will not injure the piece of awning.

OTHER SHELTERS

These remarks would not be complete without a few practical suggestions for making temporary camp shelter, be it for the night or season.

IMPROVISED CAMP SHELTER BRUSH, BARK AND LOG HUTS, ETC.

It might perchance happen that you desire to stay over night, away from the camp proper, for instance, ready to pick up a fresh trail of large game, etc., on the early morn, then these suggestions might not prove amiss.

BLANKET TENT

Here only a little instruction is necessary; patience, common sense and a willing hand can accomplish much, and about all the tools needed are a good sharp axe and knife.

The supporting frames can be improvised from a tree trunk or forked branch, from which a long ridge is trailed to the ground, the larger branches serve as side walls, and the smaller ones in turn as the shingling. The only important point to be observed in their uses is that the smaller clippings of the branches be used leaves down, lapping each other, so as to turn and shed the rain or dew; always work from the bottom up, as in shingling.

The variety shown is for the selection of the woodsman. All are simple and effective. Probably the Indian Quick-up is the simplest. It consists of light saplings of any ordinary kind or length, inserted in the ground, bent over a tree or log and the ends tied with a vine, over which a blanket is thrown,

THE INDIAN
QUICK-UP

or branches laid. Here can one with a cheerful fire, rest dry and warm. True you may have a tent somewhere, but with the information this Guide imparts, you are independent of these things.

THE BRUSH TENT

THE BRUSH LEAN-TO

THE BARK SHANTY

THE LOG CABIN

PORTABLE HUNTER'S CABIN

HUNTER'S CABIN PACKED

FIRE BUILDING

Indians used to laugh at the white men because they said that they built such a big fire they could not get near it, while the Indian built a little fire and could get close to it.

Two things are essential in the building of a campfire: kindling and air. A fire must be built systematically. First, get dry, small, dead branches, twigs, fir branches, and other inflammable material; These should be gathered during the afternoon. Place them on the ground. Be sure that air can draw under it and upward through it. Next place some heavier sticks and so on until you have built the camp fire the required size. In many camps it is considered an honor to light the fire.

If the fire is to be used for cooking, it is well to confine the heat between two large logs, or, if baking is to be done on it, it is best to build an oven with large stones. But the Indians were usually content with an open fire.

Never build a camp fire too near the tent or inflammable pine trees. Better to build it in the open.

Be sure and use every precaution to prevent the spreading of fire. This may be done by building a circle of stones around the fire, or by digging up the earth, or by wetting a space around the fire. Always

A NIGHTIME CAMPFIRE

have water near at hand. To prevent the re-kindling of the fire after it is apparently out, pour water over it and soak the earth for a space of two or three feet around it. This is very important, for many forest fires have started through failure to observe this caution.

Things to remember: first, *it is criminal to leave a burning fire;* second, *always put out the fire with water or earth.*

A fire is never out until the last spark is extinguished. Often a log or snag will smolder unnoticed after the flames have apparently been conquered only to break out afresh with a rising wind.

It's wise to get a copy of the laws of your state regarding forest fires, and if a permit is necessary to build a fire, secure it, before building the fire. Do not burn firewood just because there is plenty, leave some for a return trip. Put out the campfire before leaving camp for the day.

There is something about a campfire that makes a camp seem life-like and natural. Your glowing blaze will supply you with warmth and comfort internally and externally. Here shall weird stories be told and ruddy faces discuss the sights and pleasures of the day.

HOW TO MAKE FIRE WITHOUT MATCHES

In olden times, before the Indians had matches, and even before they had the flint and steel that our great-grandfathers used for making fire, they used rubbing-sticks. Many people have tried to make fire in this manner, but few succeed. As a matter of fact, it is not a very difficult thing to do if you know how, as the Indians did. They grew so expert that they could make fire almost as quickly as we can strike a match. The easiest and surest method of doing this is to use the bow-drill. The tools necessary consist of a bow, or bent stick, about two feet long, with a stout cord attached to each end. The drill consists of a straight piece of wood pointed at each end. One end of this rests in a drill-socket, which is simply a piece of wood with a small notch in it for the top of the fire-drill. This piece of wood is held in the hand, while the other end of the fire-drill is placed in the fire-board. This consists of a thin piece of wood with small pits cut about half an inch from the edge, and with a notch extending from the edge into the middle of the pit. The cord is given a single turn about the fire-drill and then, by drawing the bow backward and forward, the drill is caused to rotate very rap-idly in the fire-board. After a short while the dust which comes out of

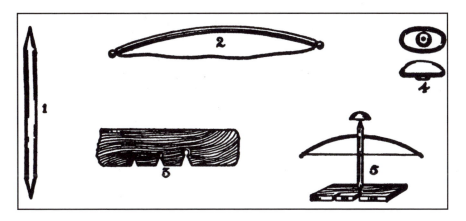

THE FIRE-DRILL

the notch grows hot and becomes a glowing coal, which can be easily ignited into a blazing fire.

Should you suddenly find yourself without dry matches or a lighter, and should the sun be high enough in the sky, a magnifying glass can be used to kindle fire by focusing the rays of the sun. Often you can use the lens of an eye-glass—so long as it is untinted. In a pinch you can even conjure up a nice little blaze with nothing but a clear glass bottle, one third full of clean water. Try it sometime, it will amaze you.

HOW TO TIE KNOTS

Every boy is familiar with rope and its uses, but not everyone is able to handle it to the best advantage. In camping and fishing, and particularly in any sport that has to do with the water, a knowledge of how to tie knots is of the greatest value and interest. Often one's very life depends on a knot holding.

A good knot has three qualities: it must be easy and quick to tie, it must hold fast when pulled tight and must be easy to untie. There are a number of knots which meet these requirements but are adapted to different uses. To learn the various knots which follow take a section of flexible rope

THE OVERHAND KNOT

THE FIGURE-OF-EIGHT KNOT

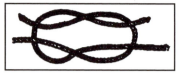

THE SQUARE OR REEF KNOT   THE FALSE REEF KNOT OR GRANNY

about four feet long and three-eighths of an inch in diameter. To keep the ends from fraying it is necessary to "whip" or bind them with twine. To do this make a loop in the twine and lay on the rope end so that the closed end of the loop projects just over the end of the rope. Begin wrapping with the long end of the twine at a point about an inch from the end of the rope, over the loop and toward the end. When you reach the end of the rope pass the free end of the twine through the loop and pull the other end of the twine. This will pull the free end under the wrapping and secure it. Cut off both ends close to the wrapping. To understand the directions remember that:

1. *The standing-part* is the long unused portion of the rope upon which the work is done.
2. *The bight* is the loop formed whenever the rope is turned back upon itself; and
3. *The end* is the part used in tying the knots.

The two primary knots are the "over-hand" and the "figure-of-eight," which must be learned first of all as a basis.

THE OVERHAND KNOT

Beginning with the position shown in the preceding diagram back the end around the standing-part and through the bight, drawing it tight.

THE FIGURE-OF-EIGHT KNOT

Make a bight as before. Then lead the end around back of the standing-part and down through the bight. The following knots are chiefly based upon these and can be easily learned by careful study of the diagrams. With practice considerable speed can be obtained, but it is best to "make haste slowly."

THE SQUARE OR REEF KNOT

This is the commonest knot for tying two ropes together. It will not slip or jam if properly tied and is easy to untie.

THE FALSE REEF KNOT OR GRANNY

If the ends are not properly crossed in making the reef knot the *granny* results, a bad and insecure knot.

THE SHEET BEND OR WEAVERS KNOT

A knot much used by sailors in bending (tying) the sheet to the clew of the sail and in tying two rope ends together. Make a bight with one rope A, B, then pass the end C, of other rope up through and around the entire bight and bend it under its own standing part.

THE BOWLINE

One of the most useful of all knots. It forms a loop that will neither jam nor slip and is the only knot which will not cut itself under heavy tension. It is much used on shipboard and in rigging when a loop is desired. To tie the knot, form a small loop on the standing-part leaving the end long enough for the size of the loop required. Pass the end up through the bight around the standing-part and down through the bight again. To tighten hold the loop in position and pull the standing-part. It is important that the knot should be held firmly in one position while tying for it is apt to slip before it is tightened. To join two sections together by this knot, tie a bowline in one end, then with the other end form the small loop, then

THE SHEET BEND OR WEAVER'S KNOT

THE BOWLINE

THE HALTER, SLIP OR RUNNING KNOT

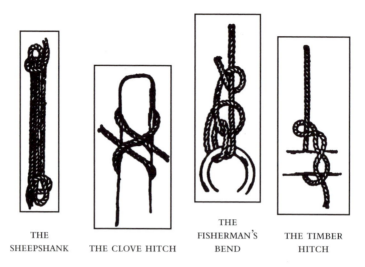

THE
SHEEPSHANK THE CLOVE HITCH

THE
FISHERMAN'S
BEND

THE TIMBER
HITCH

pass the end through the loop of the first bowline and complete the knot. This method should always be used in joining kite cord to prevent cutting.

THE HALTER, SLIP, OR RUNNING KNOT

First form a bight and then tie an overhand knot around the standing-part. An improvement in this knot for a halter knot is made by forming the overhand knot with a loop in the end which is pulled through. By pulling the end the knot is readily released.

THE SHEEPSHANK

This knot is used to shorten a rope. Take up the amount of rope to be shortened and make a half hitch around each bend as shown. If the knot is to be permanent the ends above each half hitch should be lashed.

THE CLOVE HITCH

A useful knot for quick tying and easy release. It is used in making fast the bow line of a boat coming into a wharf, in lashing poles together, etc. Hold the standing-part in the left hand and pass the rope around the pole or stake; cross the standing-part, making a second turn around

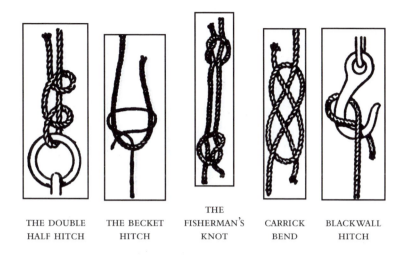

| THE DOUBLE HALF HITCH | THE BECKET HITCH | THE FISHERMAN'S KNOT | CARRICK BEND | BLACKWALL HITCH |

the pole, and pass the end under the last turn. In making a boat fast, form a bight with the end beneath, throw this over the top of the pile or mooring stake. Form another bight with the end on top, turn this over and throw over the pile, pulling ends together. This is a very secure knot which can be tied with the greatest rapidity.

THE FISHERMAN'S BEND

A useful knot for use on board a yacht. Take two turns around a spar or ring, then a half hitch around the standing-part and through the turns on the rings and another half hitch above it around the standing-part.

THE TIMBER HITCH

Much used in logging operations in hauling logs. Pass the end of the rope around the timber. Then lead it around its standing-part and bring it back to make several turns on its own part. The strain will make it hold securely.

THE DOUBLE HALF HITCH

A knot which is easy to tie and will not slip. A neat job may be had by lashing the end to the standing-part after the knot is drawn tight.

THE BECKET HITCH

Useful in fishing to bend a cord or line to a heavier cord or rope. The method is shown.

THE FISHERMAN'S KNOT

Used chiefly in tying gut. It is easy to tie and can be readily untied by pulling the two short ends. The ropes are laid alongside each other and with each end an overhand knot is made around the standing-part of the other. Pull the standing-parts to tighten.

CARRICK BEND

A knot which is used principally in joining hawsers for towing or heavy duty hoisting. Turn the end of one rope A over its standing-part B to form a loop. Pass the end of the other rope across the bight thus formed back of the standing-part B, over the end A, then under the bight at C, passing it over its own standing-part and under the bight again at D.

CAMPING GEAR ESSENTIALS

A tent or some sort of water-proof sheeting to improvise a shelter
A ground-cloth (also water-proof)
A sleeping bag, back-pack and poncho
sufficient food for meals and snacks
A good knife
A good compass, a map and flashlight
A mess-kit and canteen
A dry change of clothes
A toothbrush, bar-soap, towels
A first-aid kit
Insect repellent
50 feet of stout line or cord
Anotebook or journal, pencil and pen or marker
water-proof safety matches and/or lighters.
A good pair of boots

BLACKWALL HITCH

Used to secure a rope to a hook. The standing part when hauled tight holds the end firmly.

BREAKING CAMP

Okay, the fun's over; time to break camp and head home. Or maybe your luck's still in, and it is only time to move to another site. Either way the best campers make it their business to *leave no trace* that they were ever there.

Be sure your fire is out. Burn all wood and coals to ash.

Again, douse your fire completely, stir it thoroughly, and douse again. Then rake out the ash.

Bury all bio-degradable wastes in catholes at least 8 inches deep and well away from all water.

Pack and carry out all packaging, foils and plastics.

Make a sport of it. See just how inventive you can be in returning the site to it's natural state.

HUNTING AND FISHING

THE SHOTGUN

Choosing a Gun—Select a gun according to your game. For wildfowl *only*, a 10-gauge, 91b. gun, right barrel cylinder, left barrel choked; for wildfowl and smaller birds, select a lighter gun, preferably a 12-gauge, and if a novice, little choke is needed and more "scatter." Get the best gun your purse will stand. A cheap gun generally makes a bad shot and a disgusted sportsman.

How to Carry a Gun—The safest way is over the right shoulder, with muzzle pointing well up. The handiest way when game may be flushed is in the "hollow" of the left arm. Never carry it so that it points toward yourself, your friend or your dog.

Handling the Gun—1st, Never in excitement nor in fun point it toward any human being. 2d, Never carry it so that if accidentally discharged it would endanger life. 3d, Always think, when walking, which way your gun is pointed, and if a companion is in the field with you, no matter how near and how temptingly the game appears, do not shoot until you know just where he is, and that a stray shot may not possibly strike him, for one little pellet is sufficient to destroy an eye forever. 4th, Never get into a car or truck without taking the cartridges from the gun. 5th, Never get over a fence without either taking the cartridges out or placing the gun through the fence on the ground, so that if you fall or the fence breaks it cannot be discharged. 6th, Always carry the gun at half-cock. 7th, Never let the hammers rest on the "plungers," or pieces which strike the cap. 8th, Never try to close it when the hammers are

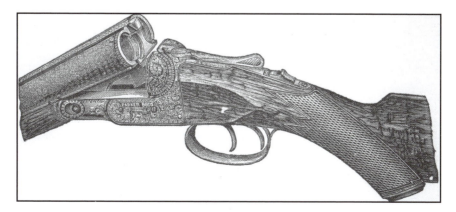

SHOTGUNS

down. 9th, Never get in front of it yourself. If you see you are about to fall, drop the gun so the muzzle will be from you. Occasionally a cartridge will stick after it has been fired. A stout, thin blade of a knife will generally extract it, if not remove the other cartridge, and then cut a straight stick and poke it out from the muzzle; but even then do not place your body in front of it. 10th, Never take hold of the muzzle to draw it toward you, nor set it up, when, if falling, its muzzle would be toward you. Finally, follow all these suggestions and be self-possessed, and the fields will afford you sport without danger.

The "Fit" of a Gun—Throw the gun to the shoulder as if to fire it. If the eye catches the center of the rib and the bead all right, the gun fits; if not, the stock is too straight or too bent. Another important point in "fit" is the length of the stock. You can't hit with an ill-fitting gun.

THE RIFLE

Hunting Rifle Qualifications—

1. safety;
2. strength, durability and ease of manipulation;
3. killing power and penetration;
4. flat trajectory;
5. portability;
6. freedom from recoil;
7. finish and ornamentation.

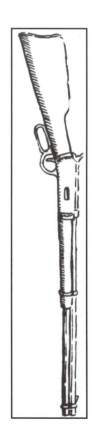

Rifle Shooting—Hold the butt firmly against the shoulder (close to the body), not on the muscle of the arm. Extend the left hand along the barrel, and hold it firmly with the fingers. The elbow should form a very obtuse angle. Press the trigger with a steady pull, but do not jerk or twitch it.

Practice in Aiming—The great desideratum in off-hand shooting is practice. If practice may not be had upon the range, good results may be attained by aiming a rifle in a room at a small object or a spot upon the wall, and snapping the hammer.

RIFLE

Aiming the Hunting Rifle—There are two methods of aiming the rifle among sportsmen: One by changing the sight taken from fine to coarse and *vice versa,* and the other by not changing the sights, but by aiming higher or lower on the target. Which of these modes is the best we don't know, each has its advocates. The best advice is probably to never vary the sight, but aim higher or lower as the case may require.

Keep Barrel Clean—Accurate shooting depends upon perfectly clean barrels. Wipe out the barrel after each shot, if possible.

First Lesson in Learning to Shoot—Go out by yourself where you can put up some object about the size of your hat, say some twenty yards away. Then take your position and commence to throw up your gun to your shoulder, and, keeping your eyes open, see how near you can bring the bead in line with your eye and the object at the instant that the butt-plate touches your shoulder. Try this a few times and then rest a few minutes. Then try again, but do not fatigue yourself. After you can throw the gun on to the mark with your eyes open, shut up both eyes and throw the gun to your shoulder in the same manner as before, and the instant that you feel the butt touch your shoulder open both eyes and see where your gun is pointed. Keep up this practice until you can throw your gun into line with any object that you may select, whether it is above, below or on the same level with your eyes.

Shoot with Both Eyes Open—Learn to shoot with both eyes open. You can see better with two eyes than with one, and the open-eyed hunter is not as apt to be a danger to himself and others.

ANIMAL TRACKS AND TRAILING

By Ernest Thompson Seton

"I wish I could go West and join the Indians so that I should have no lessons to learn," said an unhappy small boy who could discover no atom of sense or purpose in any one of the three R's.

"You never made a greater mistake," said the scribe. "For the young Indians have many hard lessons from their earliest days—hard lessons and hard punishments. With them the dread penalty of failure is 'go hungry till you win,' and no harder task have they than their reading lesson. Not twenty-six characters are to be learned in this exercise, but one thousand; not clear straight print are they, but dim, washed-out,

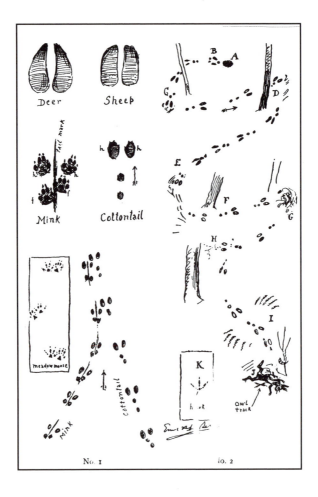

crooked traces; not in-doors on comfortable chairs, with a patient teacher always near, but out in the forest, often alone and in every kind of weather, they slowly decipher their letters and read sentences of the oldest writing on earth—a style so old that the hieroglyphs of Egypt, the cylinders of Nippur, and the drawings of the cave men are as things of to-day in comparison—the one universal script—the tracks in the dust, mud, or snow.

"These are the inscriptions that every hunter must learn to read infallibly, and be they strong or faint, straight or crooked, simple or overwritten with many a puzzling, diverse phrase, he must decipher and follow them swiftly, unerringly if there is to be a successful ending to the hunt which provides his daily food.

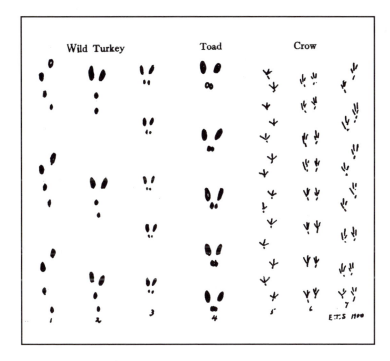

"This is the reading lesson of the young Indians, and it is a style that will never become out of date. The naturalist also must acquire some measure of proficiency in the ancient art. Its usefulness is unending to the student of wild life."

THERE ARE STILL MANY WILD ANIMALS

It is a remarkable fact that there are always more wild animals about than any but the expert has an idea of.

"Then how is it that we never see any?" is the first question of the incredulous. The answer is: long ago the beasts learned the dire lesson—man is our worst enemy; shun him at any price. And the simplest way to do this is to come out only at night. Man is a daytime creature; he is blind in the soft half-light that most beasts prefer.

While many animals have always limited their activity to the hours of twilight and gloom, there are not a few that moved about in daytime, but have given up that portion of their working day in order to avoid the arch enemy.

Thus they can flourish under our noses and eat at our tables, without our knowledge or consent. They come and go at will, and the world knows nothing of them; their presence might long go unsuspected but for one thing, well known to the hunter, the trapper, and the naturalist: wherever the wild four-foot goes, it leaves behind a record of its visit, its name, the direction whence it came, the time, the thing it did or tried to do, with the time and direction of departure. These it puts down in the ancient script. Each of these dotted lines, called the trail, is a wonderful, unfinished record of the creature's life

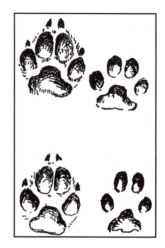

DOG TRACKS, FRONT AND BACK (½ LIFE-SIZE)   CAT TRACKS, FRONT AND BACK (½ LIFE-SIZE)

during the time it made the same, and it needs only the patient work of the naturalist to decipher that record and from it learn much about the animal that made it, without that animal ever having been seen.

It is hard to over-value the powers of the clever tracker. To him the trail of each animal is not a mere series of similar footprints; it is an accurate account of the creature's life, habit, changing whims, and emotions during the portion of life whose record is in view. These are indeed autobiographical chapters, and differ from other autobiographies in this—they cannot tell a lie. We may get wrong information from them, but it is our fault if we do; we misread the document that cannot falsify.

WHEN TO LEARN TRACKING

The ideal time for tracking, and almost the only time for most folk, is when the ground is white. After the first snow the student walks forth and begins at once to realize the wonders of the trail. A score of creatures of whose existence, maybe, he did not know, are now revealed about him, and the reading of their autographs becomes easy.

It is when the snow is on the ground, indeed, that we take our four-foot census of the woods. How often we learn with surprise from the telltale white that a fox was around our hen house last night, a mink is living even now under the wood pile, and a deer—yes! there is no mistaking its sharp-pointed unsheep-like footprint—has wandered into our woods from the farther wilds.

Never lose the chance of the first snow if you wish to become a trailer. Nevertheless, remember that the first morning after a night's snow fall is not so good as the second. Most creatures "lie up" during the storm; the snow hides the tracks of those that do go forth; and some actually go into a "cold sleep" for a day or two after a heavy downfall. But a calm, mild night following a storm is sure to offer abundant and ideal opportunity for beginning the study of the trail.

HOW TO LEARN

First—No two animals leave the same trail; not only each kind but each individual, and each individual at each stage of its life, leaves a trail as distinctive as the creature's appearance, and it is obvious that they differ among themselves just as we do, because the young know their mothers, the mothers know their young, and the old ones know their mates, when scent is clearly out of the question.

FOLLOWING THE TRACKS TO THE WATER

Another simple evidence of this is the well known fact that no two human beings have the same thumb mark; all living creatures have corresponding peculiarities, and all use these parts in making the trail.

Second—The trail was begun at the birthplace of that creature and ends only at its death place; it may be recorded in visible track or perceptible odor. It may last but a few hours, and may be too faint even for an expert with present equipment to follow, but the trail is made wherever the creature journeys afoot.

Third—It varies with every important change of impulse, action, or emotion.

Fourth—When we find a trail we may rest assured that, if living, *the creature that made it is at the other end*. And if one can follow, it is only a question of time before coming up with that animal. And be sure of its direction before setting out; many a novice has lost much time by going backward on the trail.

Fifth—In studying trails one must always keep probabilities in mind. Sometimes one kind of track looks much like another; then the question is, "Which is the likeliest in this place."

A FIRST TRY

Let us go forth into the woods in one of the Northeastern states when there is a good tracking snow, and learn a few of these letters of the wood alphabet.

Two at least are sure to be seen—the track of the blarina, or shrew, and of the deer mouse.

See the track of the meadow mouse. This is not unlike that of the blarina, because it walks, being a ground animal, while the deer mouse more often bounds. The delicate lace traceries of the masked shrew are almost invisible unless the sun is low; they are difficult to draw and impossible to photograph or cast satisfactorily, but the sketch gives enough to recognize them by.

The meadow mouse belongs to the rank grass in the lowland near the brook, and passing it toward the open, running water we may see the curious track of the muskrat; its five-toed hind foot, its four-toed front foot, and its long keeled tail, are plainly on record. When he goes slowly the tail mark is nearly straight; when he goes fast it is wavy in proportion to his pace.

THE CROSS BOW

The bow itself being made of a strong steel spring, it required the assistance of mechanical power to bend it; but the cross bow we recommend to our readers is not of quite so formidable a nature. The stock of the bow is formed

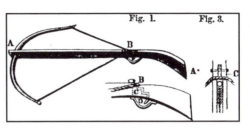

CROWBOW

something like the stock of a musket, to the extremity of this the bow is fixed; along the top of this stock a semicircular groove is formed, in

CROSS-BOWMAN

CROSS-BOWMEN

which the arrow is placed; at the near end of the stock there is a step in the wood, over this step the string of the bow is drawn, and there it remains until it is raised by means of the trigger. This last is constructed in various ways; but most often it is formed of two pieces of brass or steel or hard wood. These are let into the stock, which is pierced for that purpose; a pin is driven through the stock, and also through each of these pieces, so as to form two axles on which they can work. The effect of this arrangement is as follows: when the finger draws back the trigger, its upper portion presses against the lower half of the lever, and the upper part of that lever is consequently forced against the string of the bow, which is thus raised above the step, and being drawn forcibly forward by the bow, it carries with it the arrow.

The history of the cross-bow is very interesting. King Richard the Lion-hearted was a great cross-bowman. He carried a very strong arbalist (the old name for cross-bow) with him everywhere. Even on his long expedition to Palestine against the Saracens his favorite weapon was his constant companion. It is said that at the siege of Ascalon, Richard aimed his quarrels (the arrows of the cross-bow were called quarrels, or bolts) so skillfully that many an armed warrior on the high walls was pierced through. The steel bolts fired from the strongest cross-bows would crash through any but the very finest armor.

THE LONG BOW AND ITS USE

The bow and arrows are older than any records of history. Even the most ancient inscriptions give us no clue to their invention. Nearly all the savage tribes of men of every country and time have possessed the bow as a weapon handed down through countless generations from an unknown date.

The ancient Egyptians were archers, so were the Parthians, the Scythians and Carduchians, as well as the more savage peoples of Europe and Southern Africa.

When Columbus discovered America, the wild men of our forests were armed with bows and arrows of sufficient power and workmanship to render them quite deadly weapons, and the research of archeologists has disclosed the fact that for unknown ages before the time of Columbus, stone arrowheads were used by tribes probably long extinct when he made his discovery. So it is probable that the invention of the bow and arrow antedates every form of civilization.

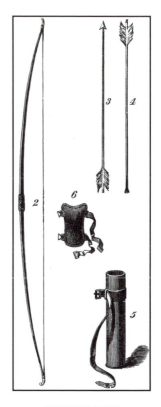

LONGBOW PARTS

1, BOW (UNSTRUNG); 2, BOW (STRUNG); 3, BARBED ARROW; 4, BLUNT ARROW; 5, QUIVER AND BELT; 6, GUARD

A LONG SHOT

It is believed that archery was practiced in Great Britain by the primitive inhabitants, though it may have been introduced by the Romans; but after the Norman conquest the art rose to its highest perfection, and England became renowned the world over for its matchless bowmen. The British archers won many famous battles, and their skill and prowess were sung by the poets and praised by historians. Even kings were proud to be able to excel with the bow.

At a very early date the wood of the yew-tree was discovered to be the best suited for bows, and the English self-yew long-bow remains to this day the historic weapon about which cluster the most romantic legends of our language. In fact, the long flint-lock rifle of the early American woodsman and the bow of the British yeoman must always remain sharply defined in the history of the world.

Shooting with the long-bow is great sport for boys, affording a most excellent physical and mental exercise and an opportunity for friendly rivalry in skill in a contest where merit always wins.

GENERAL HINTS FOR ARCHERS

1. In commencing archery never begin with a stiff bow, but select one adapted to your strength, and change this for a stronger one from time to time.
2. Never shoot with another person's bow.
3. Never put an arrow in the string when any one stands between you and the target.
4. Never talk or fool around at the time of shooting.
5. Always study to take a graceful attitude in shooting, or in moving about the field.
6. Never draw a bow near another person; as, should it snap, the danger will be greater to him than yourself.

DRAWING THE BOW

7. Never let your bow-string get untwisted or ravelled by neglect.

8. Never exhibit impatience at the tardy efforts of your fellows, or chagrin at your own failures.

9. Take care that the arrows are kept dry; otherwise they will twist and warp, the feathers will fall off, and they will soon be utterly useless.

10. Always walk *behind* the rest of the party, if you have to change your position during the shooting; and when you have shot, always go off to the left, so that your neighbor may step into your place readily, and take his turn. It is scarcely necessary to caution all young archers to refrain from crossing between the target and the shooters, at any time while archery practice is going on.

ARCHERY AT A GLANCE

Stand easily erect and firmly on both feet, with the left side toward the target.

Hold the bow in the left hand, grasping it firmly by the plush handle.

Lay the arrow across the bow on the left-hand side, just above and resting against the first "knuckle" of the left hand, and with the nock well set on the middle of the bow-string.

Hook the first three fingers of the right hand around the string, so that the string rests against the balls of those fingers, midway between the first joint and the end, with the nock of the arrow between the first and second fingers.

Now extend the left arm, turning the upper end of the bow a little to the right, and at the same time draw the string and the arrow along with it, so that at least three-fourths of the length of the shaft is taken up; here pause an instant and take aim, and then finish the draw to just below the chin, and loose.

Special care must be taken that, while loosing, the left arm maintains its position firmly and unwaveringly, and does not give way at the final moment in the slightest degree, as in this case the arrow is sure to drop short of the mark.

Bow-shooting is hard work, and is especially taxing on the strength of the left arm and the fingers of the right hand. In selecting a

Continued on next page

Continued from previous page

bow, beware of one that is too strong for easy handling. To shoot well, the archer must be master of the bow, instead of getting a bow that can master him.

Boys will find sixty yards and less the best distances for target practice.

FISHING

The "regular season" for fishing is between the months of April and November. The best time of the day for angling is, during the summer months, from sunrise to two or three hours after, and from two hours preceding sunset until an hour after that time. In the colder months the best hours are from twelve to three, for the fish are shy at biting until the air is warmed by the sun. A warm lowering day is best of all. On a cloudy day, following a moonlight night, the fish will bite readily. The most favorable winds are south and south-west—easterly, the most unfavorable.

When fishing, keep at some distance from the margin of the stream, so that your shadow may not fall upon the water, and frighten away the fish; do not indulge in laughter or loud conversation.

When the wind blows right across the water, fish with your back to the wind, as you will not only be able to throw your line better, but the fish will be on that side,

FISHERMAN

BROOK TROUT

SALMON

attracted thither by the flies and other natural bait which the wind will blow into it.

FISHING GEAR

Fishing Rods—At any place where fishing-tackle is sold, you can get rods of various lengths and fashions. The rod should, when put together, taper gradually from the butt end to the top, and be perfectly straight and even. For general purposes, a rod of about twelve feet in length is the most convenient.

Fishing Lines—Good lines should be without any irregularities. The bottom, or casting-line, for fly-fishing, which is affixed to the line on the reel, must be of about the same length as the rod; and should be strong at the top, and very fine at the "dropper," or bottom.

THE TELL-TALE JACK

Floats—These can always be gotten ready-made, in all sizes and in every variety of shape. If you prefer making to purchasing, get yourself a piece of cork, and bore a hole through it with a small, red-hot iron, then put in a quill which will exactly fit the aperture, and afterwards cut the cork so as to round its edges. When this is finished, grind it smooth with sand paper, and paint and varnish it; two or three bright colors in the painting will add much to the gayety of its appearance. The cork float should swim perpendicularly in the water, so that it may betray the slightest nibble.

Reels—A reel is very useful, as, with its assistance, parts of a river may be reached which could not otherwise be attempted; it enables the angler also to play his fish with the greatest ease and certainty. When purchasing a reel, a multiplying one should be selected-it enables the angler to lengthen or shorten his line rapidly. It must be kept clean and great care taken that no grit of any kind gets into it.

Hooks—Hooks are of various patterns and sizes. When fastening the hooks on your lines, use a strong, but fine, thread, and if you can get it near the color of your bait, so much the better.

Baits—The common angle-worm is a universal bait for fresh water angling. They grow almost everywhere except in sandy soils. The common white grub is also used successfully in trout fishing. They are found in fresh ploughed earth, and under old stumps, decaying foliage, etc. The grasshopper is also good for trout in his season. Trout or salmon spawn will attract trout quicker than any other possible bait, but it is not always to be had. Caterpillars, flies, locusts, beetles, etc., are good for trout. Live bait consists of the minnow, the shiner, and other small fish.

HOW TO OBSERVE FISH IN A BROOK

It is a very good rule to know how a creature behaves in ease and security before attempting to catch it. You must therefore try to approach without exciting attention. This is not at all difficult. Creep quietly along the bank, and you will soon get to know all the favorite lurking places of the inhabitants of the brook. You will find that when undisturbed, a fish's head is nearly always pointing up stream—that being the direction in which it expects food to come. One inference from this is sure to occur to you. If you desire to approach fish unobserved, it is best to do so by walking up stream, since in that way you come on them from behind, whereas if you walk down stream you come in the very direction in which they are looking. Still another point may be noticed. When a fish is startled and has no hiding-place near, he turns round and rushes off down stream as hard he can go. Should you be down below when somebody has frightened those above, you will observe that in their precipitate flight the fugitives spread the alarm in the pools through which they pass. Trout that were quietly feeding pop into their corners, others scurry down stream, and the few left show the liveliest signs of terror. From this it is very apparent that if you wish for any purpose to explore a number of pools and to find their inhabitants undisturbed, it is best to work up stream.

ODD MODES OF FISHING

By Daniel C. Beard

"Jugging for cats" is a most peculiar and original manner of fishing. It combines exercise, excitement, and fun in a much greater degree than the usual method of angling with the rod and reel.

The tackle necessary in this sport is very simple: it consists of five or six empty jugs tightly corked, and a stout line five feet in length, with a sinker and a large hook at the end. One of these lines dangles from the handle of each jug. Baits of many kinds are used, but a bit of cheese, tied in a piece of mosquito-netting to prevent its washing away, appears to be considered the most tempting morsel.

When all the hooks are baited, and the fisherman has inspected his lines and found everything ready, he puts the jugs into a boat and rows out upon the river, dropping the earthenware floats about ten feet apart in a line across the middle of the stream.

The jugs will, of course, be carried down with the current, and will have to be followed and watched. When one of them begins to behave in a strange manner, turning upside down, bobbing about, darting up stream and down, the fisherman knows that a large fish is hooked, and an exciting chase ensues. It sometimes requires hard rowing to catch the jug, for often when the fisherman feels sure of his prize and stretches forth his hand to grasp the runaway, it darts off anew, frequently disappearing from view beneath the water, and coming to the surface again yards and yards away from where it had left the disappointed sportsman.

One would think that the pursuit of just one jug, which a fish is piloting around, might prove exciting enough. But imagine the sport of seeing four or five of them start off on their antics at about the same moment. It is at such a time that the skill of the fisherman is tested, for a novice, in his hurry, is apt to lose his head, thereby losing his fish also. Instead of hauling in his line carefully and steadily, he generally pulls it up in such a hasty manner that the fish is able, by a vigorous flop, to tear itself away from the hook. To be a successful "jugger," one must be as careful and deliberate in

AN ACTIVE JUG

taking out his fish as though he had only that one jug to attend to, no matter how many others may be claiming his attention by their frantic signals. The illustration shows a jug turned bottom upward, the line having just been pulled by a fish taking a nibble at the bait, without having quite made up its mind to swallow it.

A very simple but ingenious contrivance for fishing through the ice may be arranged by fastening at the end of a light rod, a foot or two in length, a small signal-flag; a piece of any bright-colored cloth answers the purpose. This rod is bound with strong string to a second stick, which is placed across the hole, lying some inches upon the ice at either side; the flag, also, rests on the ice, leaving a short piece of the flag-rod projecting over the cross-stick; to this short end the line and hook are fastened. The hook is baited with a live minnow, and lowered through the hole. The tackle is then in readiness. When the fish is hooked, his struggles keep the flag flying. If the "nibble" proves a strong one and the fish is caught, the flag waving from the upright staff will signal the young fisherman, who by this easily contrived and automatic fishing-tackle may be able to attend to a number of lines if the holes are within sight from one another.

USING YOUR BARE HAND

As you proceed upward the brook grows narrower, till at last you can jump quite easily from bank to bank. Long grass and rushes and ferns at places quite hide the water from view. Still, as it ripples past some smooth close cropped hill pasture it forms little pools half-filled with big stones. These are tenanted by a variety of inhabitants, but the one most likely to arouse your curiosity is a trout four or five inches long, who darts into a hiding place at your approach. Now the problem is how to catch him alive and unhurt, with no implements save those given you by nature. It will probably take you a long time to do so, for at first you make ineffectual efforts to seize him by force, routing him out of his corner and chasing him about the water. Then you begin to call on your brains for help. First look at the little channel through which the water goes away; were the trout to become desperate he might be able to splash down it into the larger pool below, so it may be as well to stop his egress by making a wall of small pebbles. Next look where he has been playing hide and seek with you amongst the stones, and it will not be difficult to pitch on a cavity which has an entrance and an exit, either of which is easily covered with one of your hands. But he may possibly avoid it, remembering how often he has been nearly trapped and captured there before.

When the trout lies by the side of a stone, or under the bank, you will find it possible to catch him if you move your hand very gradually from behind. That is how trout are tickled: you get your hand under him, and instead of being frightened or darting away at contact with it, he merely rises in the water as he feels the touch, and affords you plenty of time and opportunity to tighten your grasp.

You will find after a little practice that to procure perfectly uninjured specimens out of a pool, the most delicate and effective instrument is your bare hand.

HIKING

THREE PRINCIPLES OF HAPPY HIKING

The first of them is to *prepare well.*

Have some reasonable idea of where it is that you are hiking. Perhaps a map and compass (or GPS) would be in order.

Get your stuff together, but don't pack anything you can just as well do without. Do plan on carrying some water.

Tell someone where it is you think you are going and when you expect to return.

Hydrate.

Finish getting your gear together, and head out.

The second of them is to *hike safely.*

Don't take silly chances, or push things too hard. Show a little of the common sense and personal discipline that are the foundations of a safe and happy trek.

The third is to *leave no sign that you were ever there.*

Leave no litter of any kind along your way. If you pack it in, you pack it out.

Do no damage of any kind. Don't pick the flowers or over-handle the foliage.

Practice silence.

HIKING

STUFF TO TAKE

A day-pack, one you are comfortable with, and light as you can get it

A good pair of shoes or boots—or both, depending

Rain gear, most times just a cheap plastic poncho will do

A couple layers of shirting; there are some great new fabrics out there

Map and compass and a pencil

Pocket-knife—gotta have it

About 20 feet of thin, sturdy cord

A few high-carb snacks

A lighter—much better than matches, which are more of a fire hazard

A basic first aid kit

A whistle

Sunglasses and sun-screen

A small flash-light or head lamp

Insect repellent

Perhaps a camera

Cell phone—aw heck! Go ahead, if you must. Darn thing probably won't work anyway

MAP READING

A map is a two-dimensional representation of the three-dimensional world. All maps will have some basic features in common and the trick to map reading is all about understanding their particular "language." You'll probably end up using a variety of maps but perhaps the most useful map is a topographic map. A topographic map uses markings such as contour lines to simulate the three-dimensional topography of the land. In the U.S. these maps are usually U.S. Geological Survey (USGS) maps. Other maps that you'll find helpful are local trail maps which often have more accurate and up-to-date information on specific trails than USGS maps do.

LATITUDE AND LONGITUDE

Maps are drawn based on latitude and longitude lines. Latitude lines run east and west and measure the distance in degrees north or south from the equator (0° latitude). Longitude lines run north and south intersecting at the geographic poles. Longitude lines measure the distance in degrees east and west from the prime meridian that runs through Greenwich, England.

Both latitude and longitude are measured in degrees (°).

All maps will list their scales in the legend. Most USGS maps are either 1:24,000, also known as minute maps, or 1:62,500, known as 15 minute maps (the USGS no longer issues 15 minute maps but the maps will remain in print for some time).

MAP LEGEND

The map legend contains a number of important details:

1. Map Name
2. Year of Production and Revision
3. General Location in State
4. Next Adjacent Quadrangle Map
5. Map Scale
6. Distance Scale
7. Contour Interval
8. Magnetic Declination
9. Latitude and Longitude

CONTOUR LINES

Contour lines are a method of depicting the 3-dimensional character of the terrain on a 2-dimensional map.

Look at the three-dimensional drawing of the mountain below. Imagine that it is an island at low tide. Draw a line all around the island at the low tide level. Three hours later, as the tide has risen, draw another line at the water level and again three hours later. You will have created three contour lines each with a different height above sea level.

As you see in Figure, the three dimensional shape of the mountain is mapped by calculating lines of equal elevation all around the mountain, and then transferring these lines onto the map.

On multi-colored maps, contour lines are generally represented in brown. The map legend will indicate the contour interval—the distance in feet (meters, etc.) between each contour line. There will be heavier contour lines every 4th or 5th contour line that are labeled with the height above sea level.

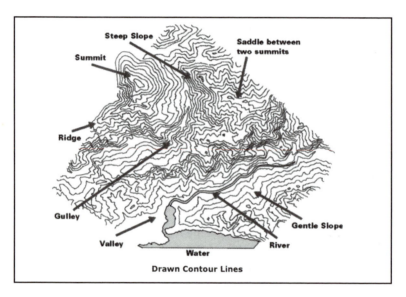

DRAWN CONTOUR LINES

- **Steep slopes** – contours are closely spaced
- **Gentle slopes** – contours are less closely spaced
- **Valleys** – contours form a V-shape pointing up the hill—these V's are always an indication of a drainage path which could also be a stream or river.
- **Ridges** – contours form a V-shape pointing down the hill
- **Summits** – contours forming circles
- **Depressions** – are indicated by circular contour with lines radiating to the center

MEASURING DISTANCES

There are a number of ways to measure distance accurately on a map. One is to use a piece of string or flexible wire to trace the intended route. After tracing out your route, pull the string straight and measure it against the scale line in the map legend. Another method is to use a compass (the mathematical kind) set to a narrow distance on the map scale and then "walk off" your route. It is a good idea to be conservative and add 5–10% of the total distance to take into account things like switchbacks that don't appear on the map. It's better to anticipate a longer route than a shorter one.

WHAT TO DO WHEN LOST IN THE WOODS

By Ernest Thompson Seton

"Did you ever get lost in the woods?" I once asked a company of twenty campers. Some answered, "Yes, once or twice." Others said, "Many a time." Only two said, "No, never." Then I said, turning to the two, "It's easy to tell that all the others here have had plenty of experience, and that you two are the tenderfeet, and have never lived in the woods."

If you spend any time at all in the wild, it is quite certain that sooner or later you will get lost in the woods. Hunters, hikers, yes, even birds and beasts, get lost at times. You can avoid it for awhile by always *taking your bearings* and noting the landscape before leaving the camp-and this you should always do-but you will still occasionally get lost and it is well to be ready for it by carrying matches, knife, and compass.

When you do miss your way, the first thing to remember is, "*You* are not lost; it is the *camp* that is lost." It isn't really serious, and it won't be, unless you do something foolish. So don't panic.

The first and most natural thing to do is to get on a hill, up a tree, or other high lookout, and seek for some landmark near camp. You may be sure of this much:

You are not nearly so far from camp as you think you are.

Your friends will soon find you.

You can help them best by signaling.

The worst thing you can do is to get frightened. The truly dangerous enemy is not the cold or the hunger so much as the *fear.* It is fear that robs you of your judgment and your limb power; it is fear that turns the passing experience into a final tragedy. Only keep cool and all will be well.

The simplest plan, when there is fresh snow and no wind, is to follow your own track back. No matter how far around or how crooked it may be, it will certainly bring you out safely.

If you see no landmark, look for the smoke of the fire. Shout from time to time, and wait; for though you have been away for hours it is quite possible you are within earshot of your friends.

If you happen to have a gun, fire it off twice in quick succession on your high lookout; then wait and listen. Do this several times and wait plenty long enough—perhaps an hour. If this brings no help, send up a distress signal—that is, make two smoke fires by smothering two bright fires with green leaves and rotten wood, and keep them at least fifty feet apart, or the wind will confuse them. Two shots or two smokes are usually understood to mean "I am in trouble." Those in camp on seeing this should send up one smoke, which means, "Camp is here."

If you have a dog or a horse with you, you may depend upon it he can bring you out all right; but usually you will have to rely on yourself.

If you are sure of the general direction to the camp and determined to keep moving, leave a note pinned on a tree if you have paper; if not, write with charcoal on a piece of wood, and also make a good smoke, so that you can come back to this spot if you choose. But make certain that the fire cannot run, by clearing the ground around it and by banking it around with sods. And mark your course by breaking or cutting a twig every fifty feet. You can keep straight by the sun, the moon, or the stars, but when they are unseen you must be guided by the compass. I do not believe much in guidance by what are called nature's compass signs. It is usual to say, for example, that the north side of the tree has the most moss or the south side the most limbs, etc. While these are true in general, there are so many exceptions that when alarmed and in doubt as to which is north, one is not in a frame of mind to decide with certainty on such fine points.

If a strong west wind, for example, was blowing when you left camp, and has blown ever since, you can be pretty sure it is still a west wind; but the only safe and certain natural compass guides are the sun, moon, and stars.

The Pole or North Star, and the Great Bear (also called the Dipper and the Pointers), should be known to every boy as they are to every Indian. The Pointers always point out the Pole-star. Of course, they go around it once in twenty-four hours, so this makes a kind of clock.

The stars, then, will enable you to keep straight if you travel. But thick woods, fog, or clouds are apt to come up, and without something to guide you, you are sure to go around in a circle.

Old woodsmen commonly follow down the streams. These are certain to bring you out somewhere; but the very worst traveling is along the edges of the streams, and they take you a long way around. All things considered, it is usually best to stay right where you are, especially if in a wild country where there is no chance of finding a farm house. Make yourself comfortable for the night by gathering plenty of good wood while it is daylight, and building a wind screen on three sides, with the fire in front, and something to keep you off the ground. Do not worry but keep up a good fire; and when day comes renew your two smokes and wait. A good fire is the best friend of a lost man.

I have been lost a number of times, but always got out without serious trouble, because I kept cool.

BASICS OF CLIMBING

A variety of techniques are used to climb different types of rock formations. The best technique stresses climbing with the weight centered over the feet, using the hands primarily for balance. Think of it as a combination of the technique required to walk a tightrope and that used to ascend a ladder.

Route Selection. The experienced climber learns to climb with the "eyes." Even before getting on the rock, he studies all possible routes, or "lines," to the top looking for cracks, ledges, nubbins, and other irregularities in the rock that will be used for footholds and handholds, taking note of any larger ledges or benches for resting places. When picking the line, he mentally climbs the route, rehearsing the step-by-step sequence of movements that the climb will require, ensuring himself that the route has an adequate number of holds and the difficulty of the climb will be well within the limit of his ability.

PITCH PICTURE

Preparation. Boot soles should be dry and clean. All jewelry should be removed from the fingers. Watches and bracelets can interfere with hand placements and may become damaged if worn while climbing. Helmets should be worn to protect the head from injury if an object, such as a rock or climbing gear, falls from climbers above. Most climbing helmets are not designed to provide protection from impact to the head if the wearer falls, but will provide a minimal amount of protection if a climber comes in contact with the rock during climbing.

Spotting. A technique used to add a level of safety to climbing without a rope. A second man stands below and just outside of the climbers fall path and helps (spots) the climber to land safely if he should

---

CAUTION

The spotter should not catch the climber against the rock because additional injuries could result.

---

fall. Spotting is only applicable if the climber is not going above the spotters head on the rock. Beyond that height a roped climbing should be conducted. If an individual climbs beyond the effective range of the spotter(s), he has climbed TOO HIGH for his own safety. The duties of the spotter are to help prevent the falling climber from hitting the head and or spine, help the climber land feet first, and reduce the impact of a fall.

Climbing Technique. Climbing involves linking together a series of movements based on foot and hand placement, weight shift, and movement. When this series of movements is combined correctly, a smooth climbing technique results. This technique reduces excess force on the limbs, helping to minimize fatigue. The basic principle is based on the five body parts described here.

Five Body Parts. The five body parts used for climbing are the right hand, left hand, right foot, left foot, and body (trunk). The basic principle to achieve smooth climbing is to move only one of the five body parts at a time. The trunk is not moved in conjunction with a foot or in conjunction with a hand, a hand is not moved in conjunction with a foot, and so on. Following this simple technique forces both legs to do all the lifting simultaneously.

Stance or Body Position. Body position is probably the single most important element to good technique. A relaxed, comfortable stance is essential. The body should be in a near vertical or erect stance with the weight centered over the feet. Leaning in towards the rock will cause the feet to push outward, away from the rock, resulting in a loss of friction between the boot sole and rock surface. The legs are straight and the heels are kept low to reduce fatigue. Bent legs and tense muscles tire quickly. If strained for too long, tense muscles may vibrate uncontrollably. This vibration, known as "Elvising" can be cured by straightening the leg, lowering the heel, or moving on to a more restful position. The hands are used to maintain balance. Keeping the hands between waist and shoulder level will reduce arm fatigue.

Whenever possible, three points of contact are maintained with the rock. When using two footholds and one handhold, the hips and shoulders should be centered over both feet. The hips and shoulders must be centered over the support foot to maintain balance, allowing the "free" foot to maneuver.

The angle or steepness of the rock determines how far away from the rock the hips and shoulders should be. On low-angle slopes, the hips are moved out away from the rock to keep the body in balance with the weight over the feet. The shoulders can be moved closer to the rock to reach handholds. On steep rock, the hips are pushed closer to the rock. The shoulders are moved away from the rock by arching the back. The body is still in balance over the feet and the eyes can see where the hands need to go. Sometimes, when footholds are small, the hips are moved back to increase friction between the foot and the rock. Do this on quick, intermediate holds, but it should be avoided in the rest position

Climbing Sequence. These steps provide a complete sequence necessary to move the entire body on the rock.

STEP 1: Shift the weight from both feet to one foot. This will allow lifting of one foot with no effect on the stance.

STEP 2: Lift the unweighted foot and place it in a new location, within one to two feet of the starting position, with no effect on body position or balance (higher placement will result in a potentially higher lift for the legs to make, creating more stress, and is called a high step). The trunk does not move during foot movement.

STEP 3: Shift the weight onto both feet. (Repeat steps 1 through 3 for remaining foot.)

STEP 4: Lift the body into a new stance with both legs.

STEP 5: Move one hand to a new position between waist and head height. During this movement, the trunk should be completely balanced in position and the removed hand should have no effect on stability.

STEP 6: Move the remaining hand as in Step 5.

as it places more weight on the arms and hands. When weight must be placed on handholds, the arms should be kept straight to reduce fatigue.

Many climbers will move more than one body part at a time, usually resulting in lifting the body with one leg or one leg and both arms. This type of lifting is inefficient, requiring one leg to perform the work of two or using the arms to lift the body. Proper climbing technique is lifting the body with the legs, not the arms, because the legs are much stronger.

Now the entire body is in a new position and ready to start the process again.

When the angle of the rock increases, these movements become more critical. Holding or pulling the body into the rock with the arms and hands may be necessary as the angle increases (this is still not lifting with the arms). Many climbing routes have angles greater than ninety degrees (overhanging) and the arms are used to support partial body weight. The same technique applies even at those angles.

SAFETY PRECAUTIONS

While ascending a seldom or never traveled route, you may encounter precariously perched rocks. If the rock will endanger your descent, it may be possible to remove it from the route and trundle it, tossing it down. This is extremely dangerous to climbers below and should not be attempted unless you are absolutely sure there is no one below. If you are not sure that the flight path is clear, do not do it. Never dislodge loose rocks carelessly. Should a rock become loose accidentally, immediately shout the warning "ROCK" to alert climbers below.

Should a climber fall, he should do his utmost to maintain control and not panic. If on a low-angle climb, he may be able to arrest his own fall by staying in contact with the rock, grasping for any possible hold available. He should shout the warning "FALLING" to alert anyone below.

Avoid climbing directly above or below other climbers (with the exception of spotters). When more than one must climb at the same time, following the same line, a fixed rope should be installed.

Be extremely careful when climbing on wet or moss-covered rock, as friction on holds is greatly reduced.

Avoid grasping small vegetation for handholds; the root systems can be shallow and will usually not support much weight.

When climbing, the climber increases his margin of safety by selecting routes that are well within the limit of his ability. When leading a group of climbers, he selects a route well within the ability of the weakest member.

When the rock is wet, or when climbing in other adverse weather conditions, the climber's ability is reduced and routes should be selected accordingly.

WATER SPORTS

SWIMMING

GETTING WET

Having stripped the body, the bather should select the best place on the bank for going down to the stream or lake; and then proceeding cautiously but quickly, wade up to his chest, turn his head to the shore and dip. He then, as people used to say, gets his pinch over. Should he not be bold enough to proceed in this way, he should, as soon as he gets his feet wet, splash some water over his head, and go into the water more gradually and try the rapid rush and dip when he gets bolder. He must not attempt to swim or strike out till he can master the feat of going into the water up to his armpits, and till he feels himself confident.

SWIMMING AIDS

Many aids have been used for the benefit of young swimmers: water-wings fastened under the arms are the common ones; but they offer dangerous temptations for beginning swimmers to go out of their depth, and then should cramp, cold, or any other accident occur, there may be trouble. A float may be just the ticket to enable the beginner to throw out his legs and feet. A piece of rigid foam, a couple of feet in length, will be found best adapted for the purpose.

The best aid to a young swimmer is a judicious friend, himself a good swimmer, who will hold him up, when he strikes off. The safest plan of all is for the learner to advance gradually up to his arm-pits in the water, and then turning about, to strike slowly out toward the shore, taking care to keep his legs well up from the bottom.

STRIKING OFF AND SWIMMING

In striking off, the learner, having turned himself to the shore, as before recommended, should fall toward the water gently, keeping his head and neck perfectly upright, his breast advancing forward, his chest inflated; then, withdrawing the legs from the bottom, and stretching them out, strike the arms forward in unison with the legs. The back can scarcely be too much hollowed, or the head too much thrown back, as those who do otherwise will swim with their feet too near the surface, instead of allowing them to be about a foot and a half deep in the water. The hands should be placed just in front of the breast, the fingers pointing forward and kept close together, with the thumbs to the edge of the fore-fingers: the hands must be made rather concave on the inside. In the stroke of the hands, they should be carried forward to the utmost extent, they should next be swept to the side, at a distance from, but not lower than the hips; and should then be drawn up again, by bringing the arms toward the side, bending the elbows upward and the wrists downward, so as to let the hands hang down while the arms are raising them to the first attitude.

HOW TO MANAGE THE LEGS

The legs, which should be moved alternately with the hands, must be drawn up with the knees inward, and the soles of the feet inclined outward; and they should then be thrown backward, as widely apart from each other as possible. These motions of the hands and legs may be practiced out of the water; and whilst exercising the legs, which can only be done one at a time, the learner may rest one hand on the back of a chair to steady himself, while he moves the opposite leg. When in the water, the learner must take care to draw in his breath at the instant that his hands, descending to his hips, cause his head to rise above the surface of the water; and he should exhale his breath at the moment his body is propelled forward through the action of the legs.

THE DOG PADDLE

In this motion each hand and foot is used alternately, as a dog uses them when swimming, as the term implies. The hands are alternately drawn toward the chin in a compressed form, and then expanded and slightly hollowed, with fingers close, and, as they strike the water, the feet are likewise drawn toward the belly, and struck backward with a kind of kick. This mode of swimming is of use to relieve the swimmer, from time to time, when going a distance.

SWIMMING UNDER WATER

When under the water, the swimmer may either move in the usual way, or keep his hands stretched before him, which will enable him to cut the water more easily, and greatly relieve his chest. If he observes that he approaches too near the surface of the water, he must press the palms of his hands upward. If he wishes to dive to the bottom, he must turn the palms of his hands upward, striking with them repeatedly and rapidly whilst the feet are reposing; and when he has obtained a perpendicular position, he should stretch out his hands like feelers, and make the usual movement with his feet, then he will descend with great rapidity in the bottom. It is well to accustom the eyes to open themselves under the water, at least in those beds of water that admit the light, as it will enable the swimmer to ascertain the depth of water he is in.

SWIMMING ON THE SIDE

In this, the body is turned either on the left or right side, while the feet perform their usual motions. The *arm from under* the shoulder stretches itself out quickly, at the same time that the feet are striking. The other arm strikes at the same time with the impelling of the feet. The hand of the latter arm begins its stroke on a level with the head. While the hand is again brought forward in a flat position, and the feet are contracted, the stretched-out hand is, while working, drawn back toward the breast, not so much impelling as sustaining. As swimming on the side presents to the water a smaller surface than on the waist, when rapidity is required, this is often preferable.

THE BACK FLOAT

The body is laid horizontally on the back, the head is bent backward as much as possible, the arms are stretched out over the head in the direction of the body, the feet are left to their natural position; if they sink, the loins must be kept as low as possible. In this position, the person, which is specifically lighter than water, remains, and may float at pleasure. The lungs should be kept inflated, that the breast may be distended, and the circumference of the body augmented. In order not to sink while in the act of taking breath, which the greater specific weight of the body would effect, the breath must be quickly expelled, and as quickly drawn in again, and then retained as long as possible; for, as the back is in a flat position, the sinking, on account of the resistance of the water, does not take place so rapidly but the quick respiration will restore the equilibrium before the water reaches the nose.

TREADING WATER

This is a perpendicular position of the swimmer, and is of great use to enable him to save a person from drowning. It is in general thought to be extremely difficult, but it is very easy. There are two ways of performing the action: in the first the hands are compressed against the hips, and the feet describe their usual circle; the other mode consists in not contracting both legs at the same time, but one after the other, so that while the one remains contracted the other describes a circle. In this mode, however, the legs must not be stretched out, but the thighs are placed in a distended position, and curved as if in a half-sitting posture.

THE FLING

The swimmer lays himself flat upon his waist, draws his feet as close as possible under the body, stretches his hands forward, and, with both feet and hands beating the water violently at the same time, raises himself out of the water. In this manner one may succeed in throwing one's self out of the water as high as the hips. This exercise is very useful, for saving one's self by catching a rope or any other object that hangs from above the surface of the water, or from any perpendicular height.

SWIMMING ON THE BACK

In this the swimmer turns upon his back in the water by the combined motion of the arm and leg, and extending his body, his head being in a line with it, so that the back and upper part of the head may be immersed, while the face and breast are out of the water. The hands should be placed on the thighs straight down, and the legs moved as in forward swimming, taking care that the knees do not rise above the surface in striking them out. Sometimes the hands are used after the motion of a wing or fan, by which a slight progression is also made at the same time that the surface of the body is well lifted out of the water.

THRUSTING

In the thrust the swimmer lies horizontally upon his waist, and makes the common motions in swimming. He then simply stretches one arm forward, as in swimming on the side, but remains lying upon the waist, and, in a widely-described circle, he carries the other hand, which is working under the breast, toward the hip. As soon as the arm has

completed this motion, it is lifted from the water in a stretched position, and thrown forward in the greatest horizontal level, and is then
sunk into the water; while the swimmer thus stretches forth the arm,
he, with the other hand stretched as wide as possible, describes a small,
circle, in order to sustain the body; after this he brings his hand in a
largely described circle rapidly to the hip, lifts the arm out of the water,
and *thrusts* it forward. During the describing of the larger circle the feet
make their movements. To make the thrust beautifully, a considerable
degree of practice is required. This mode of swimming is useful where
a great degree of rapidity is required for a short distance.

THE MILL

The swimmer lays himself on his back, and contracts himself so that
the knees are brought almost to the chin, and while one of the hands
keeps the equilibrium by describing circles, the other continues working. Thus the body is kept turning round more or less rapidly.

THE WHEEL BACKWARD AND FORWARD

In the *forward wheel* the hands are put as far backward as possible, and
so pressed against the water that the head is impelled under the surface, and the feet, by a pressure of the hands in a contrary direction, are
rapidly flung above the head, which in this manner is rapidly brought
again to the surface.

In the *backward wheel* the swimmer lies upon his back, he contracts himself, the hands, stretched forward, as far as possible, describe rapidly small circles, the feet rise, and as the point of equilibrium has been brought as near as possible to the feet, the head sinks and the feet are thrown over.

SWIMMING WITH ONE HAND

The learner, to do this, swims on one side, keeps his feet somewhat deeply *sunk*, while the arm, which in the mean time ought to work, is kept quiet—and might even be taken out of the water. It is a good practice of strength to carry, first under and then over the water, a weight of four or eight pounds.

THE CRAWL

In this process the right hand is lifted out of the water from behind, swung forward through the air with a kind of circular sweep, to the extent of its reach forward, then dropped into the water edgeways, and immediately turned—with the palm a little hollowed—downward, the body being at the same time thrown a little on one side, and the right leg struck out backward to its full extent. The hand descends toward the thigh, and then passes upward through the water in a kind of curve toward the surface. The left hand and leg perform a similar movement alternately with the right, and the measure of progression attained by these combined similar movements is very considerable.

WATER RESCUE

By Wilber E. Longfellow, United States Volunteer Life Saving Corps

READY TO RESCUE

For physical development the breast stroke is useful, for it is one that is used in carrying a tired swimmer and is used to go to the bottom for lost articles and to search for a person who has sunk before help has reached him. It is possible, you know, to go to the bottom and bring a body to the surface and swim with it to shore before life is extinct and to restore consciousness by well-directed efforts. The body of an unconscious person weighs little when wholly or partially submerged, and in salt water weighs less than in fresh water, and is consequently more readily carried. Training makes even a small boy the equal or superior of an untrained boy much larger and of greater strength, and the way to learn to carry a drowning person is to carry a boy who is not drowning to get used to handling the weights. A little struggle now and then lends realism to the work and increases the skill.

FLOATING

After the breast stroke is learned, floating on the back for rest and swimming on the back, using feet only for propulsion, leaving the hands free to hold a drowning person, should be learned. This can be readily acquired with a little practice, carrying the hands on the surface of the water, arms half bent, with the elbows close to the sides at the waist line. To carry a man this way the hands are placed at either side of the drowning man's head and he is towed floating on his back, the rescuer swimming on his back, keeping the other away. It is well to remember to go with the tide or current, and do not wear your strength away opposing it. Other ways of carrying are to place the hands beneath the arms of the drowning man, or to grasp him firmly by the biceps from beneath, at the same time using the knee in the middle of his back to get him into a floating position, the feet acting as propellers.

METHODS WHICH ENABLE THE RESCUER'S USE OF ONE ARM IN ADDITION TO THE FEET

In the first, the swimmer approaches the drowning person from the back, passes the left arm under the other's left arm, across in front of the chest, and firmly grasps the right arm, either by the biceps or below the elbow, giving him control. This leaves the right arm to swim with. The other one-arm hold mentioned is one in which the rescuer passes an arm over the shoulder of the one to be carried, approaching from the back as before, and getting a hold under the other's arm, which makes the drowning man helpless. The breast stroke carry previously mentioned is used only for helping a tired swimmer, and one in possession of his faculties who will not try to grasp the rescuer. The tired swimmer lies on the back and, extending his arms fully in front, rests a hand on either shoulder of the swimmer who rests facing him in the regular breast position allowing the feet of the other to drop between his own. Quite good speed can be made in this way, and all of these methods are practical as a trial will show. A little practice will enable the beginner to see which he can do most readily and then he can perfect himself in it for instant use.

BREAKING "DEATH GRIPS"

If one uses care in approaching a frightened or drowning person in the water, there will be no use for the release methods; but the best of

HEAD CARRY—SWIM ON BACK

swimmers get careless at times and all swimmers need to know how to get clear when gripped.

WRIST GRIP

Of these the simplest is the one where the wrists of the swimmer have been grasped by the drowning man in his struggles. The swimmer throws both hands above his head which forces both low in the water and then turns the leverage of his arms against the other's thumbs, breaking the hold easily. It should be borne in mind that a drowning man grasps what he can see above the surface of the water, so he will

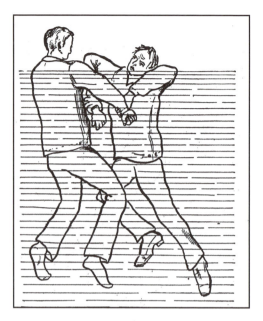

BREAK FOR WRIST HOLD

BREAKING FRONT STRANGLE HOLD

not attempt to grasp his rescuer below the points of the shoulders. Remember also that a tall man and a short man would have about the same amount of their body projecting above the surface of the water.

NECK GRIP

For the grip around the swimmer's neck from the front, for both arms around the shoulders, and for a grip in which the drowning man had the other over one shoulder and under the other arm, the break is much the same. As soon as the rescuer feels the hold, he covers the other's mouth with the palm of his hand, clasping the nostrils tightly between his first two fingers, at the same time pulling the drowning man to him with the left hand in the small of the back, treading water in the meantime. Then, taking a full breath, he applies his knee in the other's stomach, forcing him to expel the air in his lungs and at the same time preventing him from getting more by pressure on the nostrils and mouth. Should the pressure of the grip around the body be too great to allow freedom of the arms, the preliminary move in that case would be to bring both arms to the level of the shoulder, thus sliding the other's arms to the neck, leaving the rescuer's arms to cover the nose.

BACK STRANGLE

The back strangle hold is an awkward one to break and one which must be broken without an instant's delay, or the would-be rescuer himself will be in great need of help. In practice it will be found that, by grasping the encircling arms at the wrists and pushing back with the buttocks against the other's abdomen, room to slip out can be obtained. In a life and death struggle, sharper measures are needed, and if the rescuer throws his head suddenly back against the nose of the drowning man, he will secure his freedom very readily and have him under control by the time he has recovered from his dazed condition.

RESCUE FROM SHORE OR BOAT

It is not always necessary to go into the water to attempt a rescue, and in many cases, when some one has fallen off a bridge or dock, a line or buoy or boat can be used to advantage without placing more lives in danger than the one in the water. Discretion in cases like this is not a bad idea; rather than too much recklessness in swimming out, practice throwing a life buoy.

DIVING FROM THE SURFACE

When a victim from a boating accident sinks to the bottom of a river or pond of from seven to twenty feet in depth, prompt rescue methods may bring him to the surface, and resuscitation methods, promptly applied, will restore breath. If there is no current in the pond or lake, bubbles from the body will indicate its whereabouts directly beneath the place where it sank. Should there be tide or currents, the bubbles are carried at an angle with the streams and the searcher must go from the spot where the person disappeared and look along the bottom going with the current. When a drowning man gives up his struggle and goes down, his body sinks a little way and is brought up again by the buoyancy within it and the air is expelled. It sinks again and next rises less high and air is again expelled. This happens several times until enough water is taken into the stomach and air passages to offset the floating capacity. The floating capacity is barely overcome, so the body weighs but little. It is very simple, as almost any youthful swimmer knows, to go to the bottom if one can dive from a float, pier, or boat, but to be able to dive down ten feet from the surface requires practice.

DIVING FOR LOST OBJECTS

In covering a considerable area in search for bodies or lost objects, several ropes can be anchored with grapnels or rocks in squares and a systematic search thus maintained by divers. Going down from the surface is not so simple and the knack is attained by practice, especially by athletic lads. The secret is to swim to a point where a sounding is to be made, and to plunge the head and shoulders under, elevating the hips above the surface to drive the shoulders deep and give chance for a few strokes—breast stroke preferred—until the whole body in a vertical position is headed for the bottom. The elevation of the feet and lower legs in the air gives the body additional impetus downward, and when the object is attained a push-off from the bottom with both feet sends the swimmer to the surface in quick order. To carry any weight ashore, it is necessary to carry it low on the body, hugged close to the waist line, allowing one hand and both feet for swimming, or if on the back, hold by both hands using the feet as propellers.

RESTORING BREATHING

To be effective no time must be lost in getting the apparently drowned person out of the water and getting the water out of him. The Schaefer or prone method requires but one operator at a time and no waste of time in preliminaries.

When taken from the water the victim is laid on the ground face downward, arms extended above the head, face a little to one side, so as not to prevent the free passage of air. The rescuer kneels astride or beside the prone figure and lets his hands fall into the spaces between

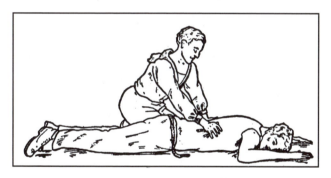

ARTIFICIAL RESPIRATION (*a*)

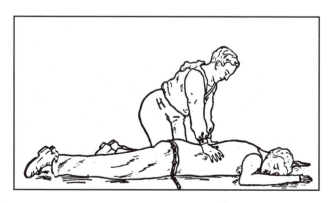

ARTIFICIAL RESPIRATION (*b*)

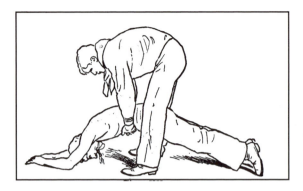

TO REMOVE WATER FROM THE LUNGS

the short ribs. By letting the weight of the upper body fall upon his hands resting on the prone man, the air is forced out of the lungs; by relaxing the pressure, the chest cavity enlarges and air is drawn in to take the place of that forced out. By effecting this change of air—pressing and relaxing, twelve to fifteen times a minute (time it by watch at first, and then count) artificial breathing is performed. Keep at it-sometimes it takes a good while before the flicker of an eyelid or a gasp from the patient rewards the life saver's efforts, and then he must carefully "piece in" the breathing until natural breathing is resumed. When breathing starts, promote circulation by rubbing the legs and body toward the heart.

Remember that by laying the patient face downward fluids in the air passages will run or be forced out and the tongue will drop forward, and require no holding.

SMALL BOATS: HOW TO RIG AND SAIL THEM

By Charles Ledyard Norton

Many persons seem to ignore the fact that a boy who knows how to manage a gun is, upon the whole, less likely to be shot than one who is a bungler through ignorance, or that a good swimmer is less likely to be drowned than a poor one. Such, however, is the truth beyond question. If a skilled hunter is now and then shot, or an expert swimmer drowned, the fault is not apt to be his own, and if the one who is really to blame had received proper training, it is not likely that the accident would have occurred at all. The same argument holds good with regard to the management of boats, and the author is confident that he merits the thanks of mothers, whether he receives them or not, for here giving their boys a few hints as to practical rigging and sailing.

The general principles of sailing are simple. If the wind always blew moderately and steadily, it would be easy and safe to sail a boat. The fact, however, is that winds and currents are variable in their moods, and as capable of unexpected freaks as the most fiery of unbroken colts, but when properly watched and humored they are tractable and fascinating playmates and servants.

The science of sailing lies in being able to manage a boat with her head pointing at any possible angle to or from the wind. Nothing but experience can teach one all the niceties of the art, but a little aptitude and address will do to start with, keeping near shore and carrying little sail.

I will suppose that the reader has the use of a broad flat-bottomed boat, without any rudder. She can not be made to work like a racing yacht under canvas, but lots of fun can be had out of her.

Do not go to any considerable expense at the outset. Procure an old sheet, six or eight feet square, and experiment with that before spending your money on new material. If it is a sheet, and somewhat weak in its texture, turn all the edges in and sew them, so that it shall not give way at the hems. At each corner, sew on a few inches of strong twine, forming loops at the angles. Sew on, also, eyelets or small loops along the edge which is intended for the luff of the sail, so that it can be laced to the mast.

You are now ready for your spars, namely, a mast and a "sprit," the former a couple of feet longer than the luff of the sail, and the latter to be cut off when you find how long you want it. Let these spars be of

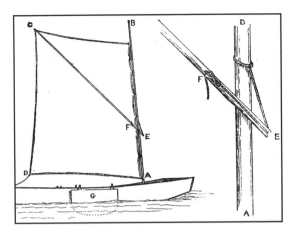

A SIMPLE RIG

pine, or spruce, or bamboo, as light as possible, especially the sprit. An inch and a half diameter will do for the mast, and an inch for the sprit. To "step" the mast, bore a hole through one of the thwarts (seats) near the bow, and make a socket, or step, on the bottom of the boat, just under the aforesaid hole—or if anything a trifle farther forward—to receive the foot of the mast. This will hold the mast upright, or with a slight "rake" aft.

Lace the luff of the sail to the mast so that its lower edge will swing clear by a foot or so of the boat's sides. Make fast to the loop at D a stout line, ten or twelve feet long. This is called the "sheet," and gives control of the sail. The upper end of the sprit, C E, is trimmed so that the loop at C will fit over it but not slip down. The lower end is simply notched to receive a short line called a "snotter," when the sprit is pushed upward in the direction of C, the sail will stand spread out. The line is placed in the notch at E and pulled up until the sail sits properly, when it is made fast to a cleat, or to a cross-piece at F. This device is in common use and has its advantages; but a simple loop for the foot of the sprit to rest in is more easily made and will do nearly as well. H is an oar for steering. Having thus described the simplest rig possible, we may turn our attention to more elegant and elaborate, but not always preferable outfits.

Make your first practical experiment *with a small sail and with the wind blowing toward the shore.* Row out a little way, and then sail in any direction in which you can make the boat go, straight back to shore if you can, with

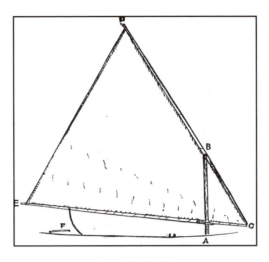

THE LATEEN RIG

the sail out nearly at right angles with the boat. Then try running along shore with the sheet hauled in a little, and the sail on the side nearest the shore. You will soon learn what your craft can do, and will probably find that she will make very little, if any, headway to windward. This is partly because she slides sidewise over the water. To prevent it you may use a "lee-board"—namely, a broad board hung over the side of the boat (G). This must be held by stout lines, as the strain upon it is very heavy. It should be placed a little forward of the middle of the boat. It must be on the side away from the wind,—the lee side,—and must be shifted when you go about. Keels and center-boards are permanent contrivances for the same purpose, but a lee-board answers very well as a makeshift, and is even used habitually by some canoeists and other boatmen.

In small boats it is sometimes desirable to sit amidships, because sitting in the stern raises the bow too high out of water; steering may be done with an oar over the lee side or with "yoke-lines" attached to a cross-piece on the rudder-head, or even to the tiller. In this last case, the lines must be rove through rings or pulleys at the sides of the boat opposite the end of the tiller. When the handle of the oar H—or the tiller F, if a rudder is used—is pushed to the right, the boat will turn to the left, and *vice versa*. The science of steering consists in knowing when to push and how much to push—very simple, you see, in the statement, but not always so easy in practice.

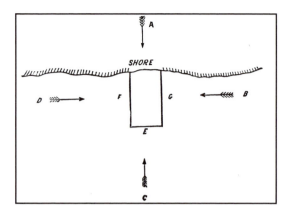

MAKING A LANDING

The sail should be so adjusted in relation to the rest of the boat that, when the sheet is hauled close in and made fast, the boat, if left to herself, will point her head to the wind like a weather-cock, and drift slowly astern. If it is found that the sail is so far forward that she will not do this, the fault may be remedied by stepping the mast farther aft, or by rigging a small sail near the stern. This is called a "steering-sail," and is especially convenient in a boat whose size or arrangement necessitates sitting amidships. It may be rigged like the mainsail, and when its sheet is once made fast will ordinarily take care of itself in tacking.

Remember that if the wind freshens or a squall strikes you, the position of safety is with the boat's head to the wind. When in doubt what to do, push the helm down (toward the sail), and haul in the slack of the sheet as the boat comes up into the wind. If she is moving astern, or will not mind her helm—and of course she will not if she is not moving—pull her head around to the wind with an oar, and experiment cautiously until you find which way you can make her go.

In making a landing, always calculate to have the boat's head as near the wind as possible when she ceases to move, whether you lower your sail or not.

If you have no one to tell you what to do, you will have to feel your way slowly and learn by experience; but, if you have nautical instincts, you will soon make your boat do what you wish her to do, as far as she is able. *But first learn to swim before you try to sail a boat.*

Volumes have been written on the subject briefly treated in these few pages, and it is not yet exhausted. The hints here given are safe ones to follow, and will, it is hoped, be of service to many a young sailor in many a corner of the world.

CAUTIONS

1. Keep the decks clear.
2. Coil up all ropes; and have a place for every thing, and every thing in its place.
3. Take care that in tacking or jibing the boom does not knock you overboard.
4. Stand clear of ropes' ends and blocks flying about, when you are hading, and the sails shaking.
5. Keep a good look-out ahead, and also for squalls, which may generally be observed to windward.
6. Always obey the orders of the steersman promptly.
7. Keep all your standing rigging taut.
8. When the boat is on the wind, sit on the weather side.
9. Wear a life preserver or life-line.
10. Should your sailboat capsize, get clear of the rigging, but try and stay with the boat. This greatly increases your chances of being rescued.

The young yachtsman should on no account attempt to take command of a boat till he is thoroughly experienced, and should never go in one without having at least one experienced hand on board; he should always have his eyes open to what is going on, and be ever ready to lend assistance promptly.

ROW BOATS AND ROWING

A *boat* is properly a vessel propelled by oars. In a larger sense the word is applied to other small vessels, which differ in construction and name, according to the services in which they are employed. Thus they are

COMMENCEMENT OF THE PULL

light or strong, sharp or flat-bottomed, open or decked, according to whether they are intended for swiftness or burden, deep or shallow water, etc.

The *barge* is a long, light, narrow boat, employed in harbors, and unfit for sea. The *long boat* is the largest boat belonging to a ship, generally furnished with two sails, and is employed for cruising short distances, bringing the cargo and bales on board, etc.

The *launch* is more flat-bottomed than the long boat, which it has generally superseded. The *pinnace* resembles the barge, but is smaller. The *cutters* of a ship are broader and deeper than the barge or pinnace, and are employed in carrying light articles, single passengers, etc., on board.

Yawls are used for similar purposes to the barge and pinnace. A *gig* is a long, narrow boat, used for expedition, and rowed with six or eight ears. The *jolly boat* is smaller than a yawl, and is used for going on shore. A merchant ship seldom has more than two boats—a long boat and a yawl.

A *wherry* is a light, sharp boat, used in a river or harbor for transporting passengers. A *punt* is a flat-bottomed boat, chiefly used for fishing on a fresh-water river. A *skiff* is a small sharp-nosed boat, used in rivers. A *dingy* is a very small stiff boat used by yachts. A *yacht* is a pleasure sailing-boat. A *lugger* is a boat furnished with sails of a peculiar cut. A *funny,* called in the West a *skiff,* is a little boat with her bow and stern nearly alike. When the bow and stern are both square, this is called a *scow.* A *bateau* and *punt* are the same. A *canoe* is a long, narrow boat hollowed out of the trunk of a tree. It is sometimes made by stretching birch bark on light ribs of tough and flexible wood. In the West the Mandan tribes of Indians used one covered with skins and nearly round. This was also used by the ancient Britons, and called a *coracle.*

RETURN OF THE SCULLS

The oar must be held firmly in both hands, grasping it between the thumbs and fingers. The whole art consists in the crew moving backward and forward together, called "swinging," and laying hold of the water as well as they can, taking care to avoid pulling in the air with great force when there is a trough or interval between two waves, and on the other hand equally avoiding a heavy wave, which has a tendency to dash the oar out of the hand. All this requires practice in the rowers, and also in the steersman, called the cockswain, who should watch for the high waves, and warn his men when a heavy one is coming. He should also take care to cross the roll of the sea as much as possible, so as to avoid being struck on the side of the boat called "the counter," which would either swamp her or else knock the oars out of the oarlocks.

COMMON ROWING ERRORS

Catching Crabs—This term implies the act of falling backward from the seat, through not taking hold of the water in the attempt to pull. *Not Keeping Time*—Independent of the awkwardness of the appearance. Not keeping time, recollect, is not putting your oar into the water at the same time as the stroke oar.

Not Keeping Stroke—This, be it observed, is totally different from the preceding fault. It is not doing work at the same time as the stroke oar. It is yet the most destructive fault that can be committed; for it must be evident that the speed of the boat depends upon the simultaneous and equal effort of its whole

Continued on next page

Continued from previous page

crew. Recollect, therefore, that the pull should commence the moment the blade is properly immersed in the water.

Doubling the Body over the Oar at the end of the Stroke—This prevents the shooting of the arms and body simultaneously forward.

Jerking is a fault to which boys who are powerful in the arms are particularly susceptible; as instead of throwing the body gradually back, and thus partially pulling by their weight, they depend solely upon the muscles of their arms. They, therefore, give a violent muscular effort, and the stroke ends, as it were, too soon, producing a jerk, which destroys the uniform propulsive power of the boat, and ultimately tires out the man. It is very annoying to the other members of the crew.

Throwing up water in rowing—This is excessively annoying to those on the same side of the boat.

Rowing with a round back—Another very common fault because considerable loss of power is the consequence.

PADDLING A CANOE

The birch-bark canoe is the boat of many of the North American Indians, and our modern canoes are made, with some variations, on the Indian model.

Many accidents happen in canoes—not because they are unsafe when properly handled, but because they are unsafe when improperly handled—and many people do not take the trouble even to find out the proper way of managing a canoe. Many canoes have seats almost on a level with the gunwale, whereas, properly speaking, the only place to sit in a canoe is on the bottom; for a seat raises the body too high above the centre of gravity and makes the canoe unsteady and likely to upset. It is, however, difficult to paddle while sitting in the bottom of a canoe, and the best position for paddling is that of kneeling. The size of the single-blade paddle should be in proportion to the size of the boy who uses it—long enough to reach from the ground to the tip of his nose. The bow paddle may be a little shorter. The canoeman should learn to paddle equally well on either side of a canoe. When paddling on the left side the top of the paddle should be held by the right hand, and the left hand should be placed a few inches above the beginning of the blade. The old Indian stroke, which is the most approved modern method for all-round canoeing, whether racing or cruising, is made with the arms almost straight—but not stiff—the arm at the top of the paddle bending only slightly at the elbow. This stroke is really a swing from the shoulder, in which there is little or no push or pull with the arm. When paddling on the left side of the canoe the right shoulder swings forward and the whole force of the body is used to push the blade of the paddle through the water, the left hand acting as a fulcrum. While the right shoulder is swung forward, the right hand is at the same time twisted at the wrist so that the thumb goes down; this motion of the wrist has the effect of turning the paddle around in the left hand—the left wrist being allowed to bead freely—so that, at the end of the stroke, the blade slides out of the water almost horizontally. If you should twist the paddle in the opposite direction it would force the head of the canoe around so that it would travel in a circle. At the recovery of the stroke the right shoulder swings back and the paddle is brought forward in a horizontal position, with the blade almost parallel to the water. It is swung forward until the paddle is at right angles across the canoe, then the blade is dipped edgewise with a slicing motion and a new stroke begins. In paddling on the right side of the canoe

CANOEING STROKE (*a*)   CANOEING STROKE (*b*)

the position of the two hands and the motion of the two shoulders are reversed.

Something should also be said about double paddles—that is, paddles with two blades—one at each end—as their use is becoming more general every year. With the double paddle a novice can handle a canoe head on to a stiff wind, a feat which requires skill and experience with a single blade. The doubles give greater safety and more speed and they develop chest, arm and shoulder muscles not brought into play with a single blade. The double paddle is not to be recommended to the exclusion of the single blade, but there are many times when there is an advantage in its use.

In getting in or out of a canoe it is especially necessary to step in the very center of the boat; and be careful never to lean on any object—such as the edge of a wharf—outside of the boat, for this may capsize the canoe. In getting out, put down your paddle first, and then, grasping the gunwale firmly in each hand, rise by putting your weight equally on both sides of the canoe.

When it is necessary to cross the waves in rough water, always try to cross them "quartering," at an oblique angle. Crossing big waves at right angles is difficult and apt to strain a canoe, and getting lengthwise between the waves is dangerous.

In case of an upset the greatest mistake is to leave the boat. A capsized canoe will support any number of persons as long as they have strength to cling to it. A single man or boy, in case of upsetting beyond swimming distance to land, should stretch himself flat upon the bottom of the canoe, with arms and legs spread down. He can thus lie in safety for hours till help arrives. When two persons are upset, they should range themselves one on each side of the over-turned boat; and, with one hand grasping each other's wrists across the boat, use the other hand to cling to the keel or the gunwale. If the canoe should swamp, fill with water, and begin to sink, it should be turned over in the water. It is the air remaining under the inverted hull that gives the craft sufficient buoyancy to support weight.

Never overload a canoe. In one of the ordinary size—about seventeen feet in length—three persons should be the maximum number at any time, and remember never to change seats in a canoe when out of your depth.

TUBING

When I was a kid growing up in small-town western New York State, it was no big deal for a boy to get himself an inner tube. All you needed to do was go down to the local gas station and ask for one. In those days every filling station and car mechanic's shop had piles of discards out back, and they were glad be rid of them. Once you had your prize, you took it home, scrubbed it clean of grit and grime with an old rag and water from the backyard garden hose, patched any tears or leaks with your bicycle tire tube repair kit, inflated it with your bicycle pump and you were ready for an afternoon's adventure at a creek or water-hole.

Times have changed, and nowadays it is no longer quite so easy for a young man to lay his hands on an inner tube; what with the advent of self-sealing car and truck tires, and the rise of a general environmental ethos (a good thing) that obliges even "mom and pop" run gas stations to clean up their lots and not leave so much "junk" lying around out back.

But even so, it is still possible for the adventurous boy to enjoy the sport of tubing. There are several commerically available "donuts" or "biscuits" on the market today, and if their ticket prices are such as to require a loan from mom or dad for their purchase, this is not necessarily

CANOEING STROKE (*c*)

a bad thing. The very fact that the tube involves an "investment" may encourage the whole family to join in. These store-bought sporting tubes also tend to be both sturdier and more flexible in terms of the various kinds of tubing the adventurous boy might like to pursue.

TUBING VARIATIONS

On water
Simple tubing on lake, swimming-hole, or gentle stream
White-water tubing on swiftly moving river or creek
Power tubing on lake or large pond-your tube is tethered to and towed by powerboat or jet-ski
Kite tubing as above-your tube is tethered to a power-craft. At high speeds your tube may very well actually take flight or "kite."
On snow
Winter tubing is akin to sledding. The tubes themselves tend to be of a heavier construction than tubes for water sport. They have handles. Also, instead of the donut hole, the center is solid though dimpled so that the tuber's body does not drag.

WATER SKIING

Count yourself a lucky young man if the day is bright and sunny; and just over there is a lake, long pond or other goodly body of water. Should your luck hold and you can somehow get your hands on a power-boat, tow-line, life-belt and water skis, then you are set for one of summertime's great adventures.

Remember:

It takes three to water ski safely: besides the skier, there should always be two in the boat, one to tend the line and spot for the skier, another who's whole attention must be given over to safe and judicious piloting of the boat.

Everybody wears a life-belt or preserver.

Always practice good etiquette on skis and in the boat. Never cut across another's bow except at a good long distance, and never cross into another skier's lane.

Be daring on your skis or board. The worst that can happen is that you wipe-out, and that in itself is huge fun. After all, it's only water.

Water skiing is said to have first gotten its start in 1922 on Lake Pepin in Minnesota, when local dare-devil, Ralph Samuelson strapped two planks to his feet and rigged a tow-line (using his backyard clothes line) behind his new bought diesel-motor launch.

SHARK ATTACK!

The shark is usually the first that comes to mind when considering fish that attack man. Whether you are in the water or in a boat or raft, you may see many types of sea life around you. Some may be more dangerous than others. Generally, sharks are the greatest danger to you. Other animals such as whales, porpoises, and stingrays may look dangerous, but really pose little threat in the open sea.

Of the many hundreds of shark species, only about 20 species are known to attack man. The most dangerous are the great white shark, the hammerhead, the make, and the tiger shark. Other sharks known to attack man include the gray, blue, lemon, sand, nurse, bull, and oceanic white tip sharks. Consider any shark longer than 1 meter dangerous.

There are sharks in all oceans and seas of the world. While many live and feed in the depths of the sea, others hunt near the surface. The sharks living near the surface are the ones you will most likely see. Their dorsal fins frequently project above the water. Sharks in the tropical and subtropical seas are far more aggressive than those in temperate waters.

All sharks are basically eating machines. Their normal diet is live animals of any type, and they will strike at injured or helpless animals. Sight, smell, or sound may guide them to their prey. Sharks have an acute sense of smell and the smell of blood in the water excites them. They are also very sensitive to any abnormal vibrations in the water. The struggles of a wounded animal or swimmer, underwater explosions, or even a fish struggling on a fish line will attract a shark.

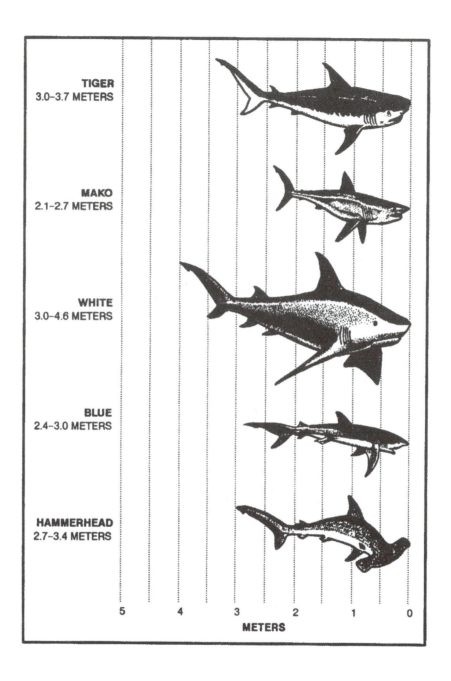

Sharks can bite from almost any position; they do not have to turn on their side to bite. The jaws of some of the larger sharks are so far forward that they can bite floating objects easily without twisting to the side.

Sharks may hunt alone, but most reports of attacks cite more than one shark present. The smaller sharks tend to travel in schools and attack in mass. Whenever one of the sharks finds a victim, the other sharks will quickly join it. Sharks will eat a wounded shark as quickly as their prey.

Sharks feed at all hours of the day and night. Most reported shark contacts and attacks were during daylight, and many of these have been in the late afternoon. Some of the measures that you can take to protect yourself against sharks when you are in the water are—

- Stay with other swimmers. A group can maintain a 360-degree watch. A group can either frighten or fight off sharks better than one.
- Always watch for sharks. Keep all your clothing on, including your shoes. Historically, sharks have attacked the unclothed men in groups first, mainly in the feet.

If a shark attack is imminent while you are in the water, splash and yell just enough to keep the shark at bay. Sometimes yelling underwater or slapping the water repeatedly will scare the shark away, but conserve your strength for fighting in case the shark attacks.

If attacked, kick and strike the shark. Hit the shark on the gills or eyes if possible. If you hit the shark on the nose, you may injure your hand if it glances off and hits its teeth.

When you are in a raft and see sharks—

- Do not fish. If you have hooked a fish, let it go. Do not clean fish in the water.
- Do not throw garbage overboard.
- Do not let your arms, legs, or equipment hang in the water.
- Keep quiet and do not move around.

When you are in a raft and a shark attack is imminent, hit the shark with anything you have, except your hands. You will do more damage to your hands than the shark. If you strike with an oar, be careful not to lose or break it.

If bitten by a shark, the most important measure for you to take is to stop the bleeding quickly. Blood in the water attracts sharks. Get yourself or the victim into a raft or to shore as soon as possible. If in the water, form a circle around the victim (if not alone), and stop the bleeding with a tourniquet.

OTHER DANGEROUS FISH AND MOLLUSKS

Common sense will tell you to avoid confrontations with hippopotami, alligators, crocodiles, and other huge river creatures. There are, however, a few smaller river creatures with which you should be cautious.

Electric Eels may reach 2 meters in length and 20 centimeters in diameter. Avoid them. They are capable of generating up to 500 volts of electricity. They use this shock to stun prey and enemies. Normally, you find these eels in the Orinoco and Amazon river systems in South America. They are bulkier than our native eels. Their upper body is dark gray or black, with a lighter-colored underbelly.

Piranhas are another hazard of the Orinoco and Amazon River systems, as well as the Paraguay River Basin, where they are native. These fish vary greatly in size and coloration, but usually have a combination of orange undersides and dark tops. They have white, razor-sharp teeth that are clearly visible. They may be as long as 50 centimeters. Use great

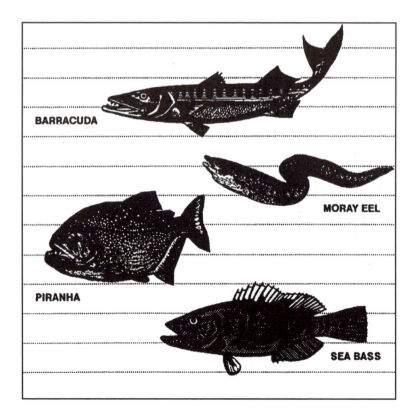

care when crossing waters where they live. Blood attracts them. They are most dangerous in shallow waters during the dry season.

Turtles Be careful when handling and capturing large freshwater turtles, such as the snapping turtles and soft-shelled turtles of North America and the matamata and other turtles of South America. All of these turtles will bite in self-defense and can amputate fingers and toes.

The **Platypus** or duckbill is the only member of its family and is easily recognized. It has a long body covered with grayish, short hair, a tail like a beaver, and a bill like a duck. Growing up to 60 centimeters in length, it may appear to be a good food source, but this egg-laying mammal—he only one in the world—is very dangerous. The male has a poisonous spur on each hind foot that can inflict intensely pain-ful wounds. You find the platypus only in Australia, mainly along mud banks on waterways.

In salt water, other ferocious fish include the barracuda, sea bass, and moray eel. The sea bass is usually an open water fish. It is dangerous due to its large size. It can remove large pieces of flesh from a human. Barracudas and moray eels have been known to attack man and inflict vicious bites. Be careful of these two species when near reefs and in shallow water. Moray eels are very aggressive when disturbed.

WINTER ACTIVITIES

CROSS COUNTRY SKIING

THE SKIS SHOULD BE KEPT CLOSER TOGETHER THAN SHOWN. THE CLOSER THE BETTER

To choose your way correctly and quickly, either up hill or down, is a most important part of cross country skiing, demanding just about as much skill as every other aspect of the sport. What is known as *an eye for country* seems to be very largely a natural gift. Some people are always in difficulties, while others, often less skilful in other respects, are able to find their way almost intuitively across unknown ground. But of course, experience in this counts for a great deal, and what may at first sight strike the beginner as prophetic inspiration is often nothing more than an application of previously acquired knowledge to present conditions. It is impossible to give much information of this kind in a book, but nevertheless, a few hints on the subject may be useful.

In the first place it may be said that as a general rule snow is in better condition on the north sides of hills, which are shaded from the sun, than on the south, which are exposed to it. Also it is true that the sun is warmer towards the middle of the day than in the early morning, but that the temperature usually falls about a degree Fahrenheit for every 300 feet you ascend. So it generally pays to climb a mountain on the south side, where the snow will be firm, and to start early in the morning. The north side will usually be the best for the descent, as there the snow will probably be powdery and manageable.

All things considered, you should learn to go slowly before you learn to go fast. As soon as you can "run" straight fairly well, you should undertake to regulate your speed and steer by means of what is known as "stemming". In practicing this movement you will at the same time learn how to balance yourself with your weight on one foot, a necessary accomplishment; for, though in cross country skiing both skis are usually kept on the ground, *your weight is nearly always mainly on one foot.*

After you have learnt something of stemming, you should not find much difficulty in acquiring some speed.

LEAN FORWARD! is the motto of the cross country skier.

Place your skis parallel, one about a foot in front of the other, and throw your body forward as much as possible; you ought to feel as if about to fall on your nose. To the onlooker you seem to be standing on the *entire* sole of the foot, but in reality all the weight rests on the front part and the toes. So, stand erect on the skis, your knees a little bent, and then lean forward without bending any part of your body (especially not the region of the hips) and without raising the heel. Don't lean back and never assume a position as if you're about to sit down, because that would press down the heel. Every violation of this rule of leaning forward is punished by the ski "bolting" from under you, often resulting in a nasty fall. Instead, slide your skis forward one after the other, taking care to shift your weight to the forward ski, then rediscover your balance as you bring forward the other ski.

WALKING WITH SKIS ON THE LEVEL

Walking with skis on the level differs from ordinary walking or skating in that *one must not strike out*, there being no fulcrum or point of resistance. Keep the skis *parallel* and *as close together as possible,* for a narrow spoor has many advantages, besides being "good form." Throw the weight of the body forward and *slide on the advanced leg;* the "hind" leg must be absolutely disengaged—that is to say, do not strike out by trying to press the snow with it. Begin with long, slow steps, lunging forward with bent knee. Do not lift the ski from the ground, but slide along regularly and conscientiously; do not hurry or flurry, but save your breath. In one's first steps one must specially cultivate precision, sliding forward with ski exactly parallel, and distributing the weight properly. Lean forward! slide!

A single stick on the level is of but little service, but with two sticks the pace can be increased, especially on a good firm surface. Both sticks should be thrown forward simultaneously, and the slide on the advanced leg accelerated by a vigorous push with both arms. When proceeding in this way it is well to observe some kind of rhythm; and, as the snow is seldom slippery enough to admit of a push at each step, one should move, for example, one, two, three steps (swinging the sticks forward), and then push with the arms, sliding on, say, the right leg; then run one, two, three steps and push, sliding on the left leg, and so on.

UP-HILL

To many people it is a matter for wonder how it is possible to climb any considerable hill at all on ski. We remember well the look of polite incredulity which passed across the face of a mountaineering friend some years ago when we told him that a certain well-known pass in the Alps had been traversed in winter. He had tried skis himself, but had made very little of them, and the pass in question is a stiff one to negotiate even in summer. But now long climbs on skis in winter have become common.

In ascending a steep incline the art lies:

1. in knowing just how steeply one can go without a slip;
2. in the correct placing of the ski in the snow; and
3. in the correct balancing of the body upon the ski when so placed. The correct placing of the skis is not a difficult matter. The secret lies in raising the point of the ski an inch or two from the ground and bringing it *straight* down with a *firm* stamp. Remember that

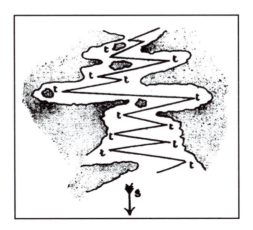

—*Climbing a slope*—*s* = THE FALL OF THE SLOPE; *t* = TURN HERE. THE SHADED PARTS ARE OBSTRUCTIONS (ROCKS, THICK GROWTH, &C.).

where the foot is brought down there it must stop. If it slips even the least tiny bit you must stamp again.

Next bring the weight forward as evenly as possible on to the ski you have stamped, and advance the other leg. In doing so take the greatest care to balance the weight of the body *straight over* the stamped ski; lean neither backwards nor forwards, or you are certain to slip.

To negotiate a steep slope one must go across and upward at a convenient angle, making a zig-zag track, as an engineer would plan a good mountain road. Turn at the corners as described, and when so doing remember to assume a safe standing position, for a slip on a steep slope may be attended by unpleasant consequences. The correct position in which to stand before turning is clearly with the ski horizontally in space—that is to say, at right angles to the direction of the gradient; then one cannot slip while engrossed in the task.

It is important when proceeding in this way to remember, when lifting the *upper* ski, *to raise its heel from the snow and place it well up-hill in a horizontal position.* Most beginners move only the front part of the ski, and place it in the snow with the heel pointing down hill. Even if the upper ski does not slip in this wrong position (as usually happens), the lower ski, when it comes to be lifted, is sure to be placed across the

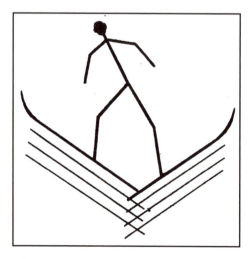

—*"Herring-boning."*—THE FIGURE IS IN THE ACT OF LIFTING THE RIGHT SKI OVER
THE HEEL OF THE LEFT. THE LIGHT LINES ARE HIS TRACKS
NOTE—SWING THE BODY WELL, AS SHOWN

*—Hill climbing sideways.—*USED ONLY ON *very* STEEP SLOPES.
THE LIGHT LINES ARE OLD TRACKS

heel of the upper ski, imprisoning it and preventing the next step being taken. You are certain to make this mistake very frequently at first.

A single pole is not of any very positive assistance up-hill, though it has a negative value on *very* steep ground both in aiding the balance and in giving a feeling of security against slipping. In traversing a slope it should be held across the body with the point touching the snow on the upper side. The beginner will also find it useful to assist him in rising to his feet after a fall. He should, however, entirely abandon all idea of pulling himself up-hill with his stick; to do so is quite impossible. Balance is what is required, plus a little thigh muscle, which will come with practice.

Two sticks are, however, of considerable help, especially on moderate slopes up which it is possible to go straight. They should be placed in the snow alternately, after the manner which nature dictates. In traversing steep ground they cease to be of service, for the lower one is not long enough to reach the slope below one's feet, and the upper one cannot be used effectively on the bank at one's side. Under such circumstances it is better, and safer, to hold them together and to use them as one, as described above.

In general for long climbs it is best to go comparatively slowly and to "keep at it." The speed of a party should be that of the slowest man. If you happen to be that unfortunate individual, don't lag behind if you can help it, but don't hesitate to shout to the others if they are going too fast for you. If, however, they are novices and persist in rushing, slow down and go your own pace. It is not at all improbable that if you go steadily you may be the first at the top, after all; but even if you arrive twenty minutes later than the others you are in no way dishonoured.

Strictly between ourselves, we rather like to be last man, and to allow our more energetic friends to go on ahead. The last man has far the easiest place on a newly made track, and we do not thirst for the glory of breaking the snow.

But, of course, a properly organized party should keep together, and its members should take it in turns to go ahead. It is in itself a pleasure to move steadily upwards in this way, the ski and the sticks keeping time, and it makes the way seem shorter and easier for everybody.

One concluding word of advice may here be given. Eat your lunch some little distance below your intended highest point. The tops of mountains and passes are apt to be draughty, and, besides, it is much better to begin the run down when the muscles are warm and supple than to wait till after they have turned cold and stiff from sitting about.

GLIDING DOWN

Gliding down is the characteristic part of ski-running, as distinct from the use of pattens, Canadian snow-shoes, etc. It is the reward reaped after the labors of the climb, the highest advantage that any physical exercise can safely derive from terrestrial attraction.

Let us imagine ourselves on the top of some long mountain ready for the plunge. There is a clear course between the steep rocks near the top, and an open run across the glacier below to the terminal moraine a mile off. We can see every yard of the way, and all is fair going, yet we feel just the merest tinge of nervousness, for the incline is steep, and looks steeper than it is. But there is really no danger, so it is over the edge and off! In an instant all fears are left behind, for now balance and quickness of eye are to be put to the test, and the wind is whistling and the snow dust spurting. We whiz past the rocks and over a few inequalities, negotiated here by a spring and a flight of a few yards through the air and there by a compensating yielding of the knees. Now we rush out on to the smooth surface of the glacier, where there is no jar and no vibration. Our feet seem to have vanished, and we lean, as it were, in space, with the ice-wind pressed against us. There is no more need for balancing, and no thought of falling, so even is the motion and so trustworthy the snow. Smoothly our wooden wings bear us onwards, and the furlongs lie behind! But the end approaches, the slope becomes less steep, the pace slackens, and presently we glide gently up the opposite slope of the moraine and turn to watch our companions.

Such is the best picture we can give you of a good straight glissade on skis; but there is not the slightest reason, friend novice, why you yourself should not enjoy the reality ere long.

BUILDING AN ICE YACHT

The body, or boat proper, is made up of three principal parts—the keel or center timber, and two side timbers. The keel is 24 feet 6 inches long, 3 inches wide, and 9 inches deep. The two side timbers are each 2 1/2 inches wide and 4 inches deep. They are joined at the stern to a semi-circle of 15 inches radius, and at the mast by means of a curved plank 12 inches wide, 3 inches deep, and 7 feet 4 inches long, which is bolted to them. The runner plank, to which the two forward runners are bolted, and which is bolted to the under side of the side timbers and running under the keel, projects about an inch below the side timbers. The runners are three in number, two forward and one aft (called the rudder), are made of 2-inch plank, and have steel shoes bolted to

them by means of bolts tapped into the shoe and running through the wood, having their heads countersunk therein so as to be flush. The shoes are fastened by 5 5/8-inch bolts tapped into them; they are ground on the running edge to an angle of 90°, and are 1 3/4 inches deep. The runner, or rudder, is smaller than the forward ones, and is fastened to a rudder post, which passes through the keel and terminates in a tiller, 2 feet 8 inches long, by which the boat is steered. The body is planked on the under side with inch boards for a distance of about 7 feet from the after end. The mast is 20 feet high, 5 inches in diameter at the foot and 3 1/2 inches at the top, and has a topmast fixed into the

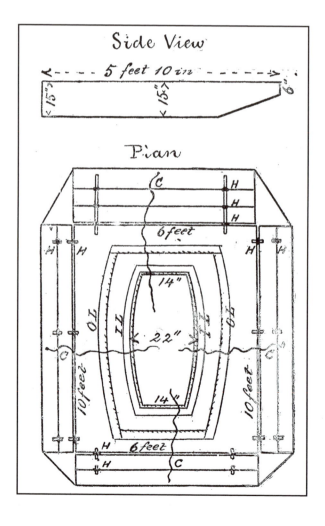

top 3 feet long, 2 inches in diameter at the large and 1 inch at the small end.

The bowsprit is 16 feet long, 6 inches deep at the widest part and 3 1/2 at the ends, and is 3 inches wide on the bottom, beveling to 2 inches on the top. It is fastened to the keel by means of an iron band three quarters of an inch wide, and also by a bolt running through both. The boom is 29 feet long, 4 1/2 inches in diameter in the center, and 2 1/2 inches at the ends. It is fastened aft of the mast by means of an eye and a staple. The jibboom is 15 feet 3 inches long, 2 1/2 inches in diameter at the center, and 2 inches at the ends, and is fastened to the forward end of the bowsprit. The gaff is 8 feet 9 inches long, 2 inches in diameter, and has the jaws made to an angle, so that they set square across the mast. The sails are two in number, the mainsail and the jib. The mainsail has the following dimensions: Hoist, 14 feet 6 inches; foot, 28 feet; head, 8 feet; leach, 28 feet; the lift of the mainsail at the end of the boom is 1 foot 6 inches. The dimensions of the jib are as follows: Hoist, 15 feet; foot, 14 1/2 feet; leach 32 feet; and it has a lift of 1 foot. The rigging is of half-inch round iron and wire rope.—*Scientific American*.

FIELD SCIENCE

AMERICAN BIRDS

BALD EAGLE

The *bald eagle* is the emblem of America. It is three to four feet from beak to tail, and six or seven feet across the wings. When fully adult it is known by its white head, neck, and tail, and brown body; but when young it is brownish black, splashed and marked with dull white.

The only other eagle found in the United States is the *golden,* or *war eagle.* This is a little larger. When full grown it is dark brown, with the basal half of tail more or less white. The plumage of the young birds is somewhat like that of the young bald eagle; but the two species may always be distinguished by the legs. The war eagle wears leggings—his legs are feathered to the toes. He is ready for the warpath. The bald eagle has the legs bald, or bare on the lower half.

The *Redtailed hawk, or henhawk.* The common hawks of America are very numerous and not easy to distinguish. The best known of the large kinds is the redtail. This is about two feet long and four feet across the wings. In general it is dark brown above and white beneath, with dark brown marks; the tail is clear reddish with one black bar across near the tip. In young birds the tail is gray with many small bars. It is common in North America east of the Rockies up to mid-Canada.

REDTAILED HAWK OR HENHAWK

It does much good, killing mice and insects. It is noted for its circling flight and far-reaching whistle or scream.

The *barred, or hoot owl* is known at once by the absence of horns, the black eyes, and the plumage *barred* across the chest and *striped* below that. It is about twenty inches long, in general gray-brown marked with white. It is noted for its loud hooting; it is the noisiest owl in our woods. It is found in the wooded parts of America up to about latitude 50 degrees, east of the Plains.

The *great horned owl, or cat owl* is the largest of our owls. About twenty-four inches long and four feet across the wings, it is known at once by its great ear tufts, its yellow eyes, its generally barred plumage of white, black and buff, and its white shirt front. This is the winged tiger of the woods. Noted for its destruction of game and poultry, it is found throughout the timbered parts of North America.

The *screech owl* is not unlike the horned owl in shape and color but is much smaller—only ten inches long. Sometimes its plumage is red instead of gray. It feeds on mice and insects and has a sweet mournful song in the autumn—its lament for the falling leaves. It is found in the timbered parts of North America.

The *turkey vulture, or buzzard* is about two and a half feet long and about six feet across its wings. It is black everywhere except on the under

(A) BARRED OR HOOT OWL; (B) GREAT HORNED OWL;
(C) TURKEY VULTURE OR BUZZARD; (D) SCREECH OWL

side of the wing which is gray, and the head which is naked and red. It is known at once by the naked head and neck, and is famous for its splendid flight. It is found from the Atlantic to the Pacific and north to Saskatchewan. It preys on carrion.

LOON
AND
COMMON SEAGULL

In the Southern States is another species—the *black vulture*, or *carrion crow*—which is somewhat smaller and wears its coat collar up to its ears instead of low on the neck.

The *loon*. The common Loon is known by its size—thirty-two inches long and about four feet across the wings—and its brilliant black-and-white plumage. It is noted for its skill as a fisher and diver. Its weird rolling call is heard on every big lake in the country.

The *common seagull* is twenty-four inches long and four feet across. The plumage is white with blue-gray back, when adult; but splashed brown when young, and with black tips to the wings. Its beak is yellow with red spot on the lower mandible. It is found throughout North America.

The *pelican* is known at once by its great size—about five feet long and eight feet across the wings—by its long beak, its pouch,

PELICAN

WILD DUCK, OR MALLARD

WOOD DUCK, OR SUMMER DUCK
AND
WILD GOOSE, CANADA GOOSE, OR HONKER

and fully webbed feet. Its plumage is white, but the wing tips are black. It is found in the interior of America.

The *wild duck, or mallard,* of all our wild ducks, is the best known. It is about twenty-three inches long. Its bottle-green head, white collar, chestnut breast, penciled sides, and curled-up tail feathers identify it. The female is streaky brown and gray. It is found in all parts of the continent, up to the edge of the forest.

The *wood duck, or summer duck* is a beautiful duck about eighteen inches long. Its head is beautifully variegated, bottle-green and white. Its eye is red, its breast a purplish-chestnut, checkered with white spots, while its sides are buff with black pencilings. This is one of the wildest and most beautiful of ducks. It nests in hollow trees and is found in North America up to about latitude 50 degrees.

The *wild goose* is a fine bird about three feet long. Its head and neck are black; its cheek patch white; its body gray; its tail black with white coverts above and below. It is found up to the Arctic regions, and breeds north of about latitude 45 degrees. It is easily tamed and reared in captivity.

The *bluejay* is a soft purplish blue above, and white underneath. The wings and tail are bright blue with black marks. It is found in the

BLUEJAY AND BOBOLINK, OR REEDBIRD

woods of America east of the Plains. The bluejay is a wonderful songster and mimic, but it is mischievous.

The *common crow* is black from head to foot, body and soul. It is about eighteen inches long and thirty wide. It makes itself a nuisance in all the heavily wooded parts of eastern North America.

The *bobolink, or reedbird* is about seven and a half inches long. The plumage is black and white, with a brown or creamy patch on nape; and the tail feathers all sharply pointed. The female, and the male in autumn, are all yellow buff with dark streaks. Famous for its wonderful song as it flies over the meadows in June, it is found in North America, chiefly between north latitude 40 and 52 degrees.

The *baltimore oriole* is about eight inches long, flaming orange in color, with black head and back and partly black tail and wings. The female is duller in plumage. Famous for its beautiful nest, as well as its gorgeous plumage and ringing song, it is abundant in eastern North America in open woods up to northern Ontario and Lake Winnipeg.

The *purple grackle, or crow blackbird* is northern bird of paradise that looks black at a distance but its head is shiny blue and its body iridescent. It is twelve inches long. When flying it holds its long tail with the edge raised like a boat, hence "boat tail." In various forms it is found throughout the eastern States, and in Canada up to Hudson Bay.

BALTIMORE ORIOLE AND
PURPLE GRACKLE, OR CROW BLACKBIRD

COMMON HOUSE WREN AND
CHICKADEE

ROBIN

The *common house wren* is about five inches long; soft brown above and brownish gray below, it is barred with dusky brown on wings and tail. It nests in a hole, and is found in wooded America east of the Plains, north to Saskatchewan, Ottawa, and Maine.

The *chickadee* is a cheerful little bird five and a half inches long. Its cap and throat are black. Its upper parts are gray, its under parts brownish, its cheeks white, no streaks anywhere. It does not migrate, so it is well known in the winter woods of eastern America up to the Canadian region where the brown-capped or Hudson chickadee takes its place.

BLUEBIRD

WOOD THRUSH

The *robin* is about ten inches long, mostly dark gray in color, but with black on head and tail; its breast is brownish red. The spots about the eye, also the throat, the belly, and the marks in outer tail feathers are white. Its mud nest is known in nearly every orchard. Found throughout the timbered parts of America north to the limit of trees.

The *wood thrush* is about eight inches long, cinnamon-brown above, brightest on head, white below, with black spots on breast and sides. The thrush is distinguished from the many thrushes in America, much like it, by the reddish head and round black spots on its under sides. It is found in the woods of eastern North America up to Vermont and Minnesota.

The *bluebird* is about seven inches long, brilliant blue above, dull red-brown on breast, white below. Found in eastern North America, north to about latitude 50 degrees in the interior, not so far on the coast.

UNDERSTANDING THE WEATHER

Weather Characteristics. The earth is surrounded by an atmosphere that is divided into several layers. Weather is a result of the atmosphere, oceans, land masses, unequal heating and cooling from the sun, and the earth's rotation. The weather found in any one place depends on many things such as the air temperature, humidity, air pressure, etc.

Air pressure is the "weight" of the atmosphere at any given place. The higher the pressure, the better the weather will be. With lower air pressure, the weather will more than likely be worse. In order to understand this, imagine that the air in the atmosphere acts like a liquid. Areas with a high level of this "liquid" exert more pressure on an area and are called high-pressure areas. Areas with a lower level are called low-pressure areas.

High Pressure. Characteristics of a high-pressure area:

- The airflow is clockwise and out, otherwise known as an "anticyclone."
- Associated with clear skies.
- Generally the winds will be mild.
- Depicted as a blue "H" on weather maps.

Low Pressure. Characteristics of a low-pressure area:

- The airflow is counterclockwise and in, otherwise known as a "cyclone."
- Associated with bad weather.
- Depicted as a red "L" on weather maps.

Air from a high-pressure area is basically trying to flow out and equalize its pressure with the surrounding air. Low pressure, on the other hand, is building up vertically by pulling air in from outside itself, which causes atmospheric instability resulting in bad weather.

On a weather map, these differences in pressure are depicted as isobars. Isobars resemble contour lines. The areas of high pressure are called "ridges" and lows are called "troughs."

Wind. In high mountains, the ridges and passes are seldom calm; however, strong winds in protected valleys are rare. Normally, wind speed increases with altitude since the earth's frictional drag is strongest near the ground. This effect is intensified by mountainous terrain. Winds are accelerated when they converge through mountain passes and canyons. Because of these funneling effects, the wind may blast with great force on an exposed mountainside or summit. Usually, the local wind direction is controlled by topography.

Humidity. Humidity is the amount of moisture in the air. All air holds water vapor even if it cannot be seen. Air can hold only so much water vapor; however, the warmer the air, the more moisture it can hold. When air can hold all that it can the air is "saturated" or has 100 percent relative humidity.

Cloud Formation. Clouds are indicators of weather conditions. By reading cloud shapes and patterns, observers can forecast weather with little need for additional equipment such as a barometer, wind meter, and thermometer. Anytime air is lifted or cooled beyond its saturation point (100 percent relative humidity), clouds are formed.

Types of Clouds. Clouds are one of the signposts to what is happening with the weather. They can be classified by height or appearance, or even by the amount of area covered vertically or horizontally. Clouds are classified into five categories: low-, mid-, and high-level clouds; vertically-developed clouds; and less common clouds.

Fronts. Fronts occur when two air masses of different moisture and temperature contents meet. One of the indicators that a front is approaching is the progression of the clouds. The four types of fronts are warm, cold, occluded, and stationary.

Weather Forecasting. The use of a portable arometer, thermometer, and wind meter, help in making local weather forecasts. Reports from other localities and from any weather service like the National Weather Bureau, are also helpful. Weather reports should be used in conjunction with the locally observed current weather situation to forecast future weather patterns.

OLD TIME WEATHER WISDOM

When the dew is on the grass,
Rain will never come to pass.
When the grass is dry at night,
Look for rain before the light.
When grass is dry at morning light,
Look for rain before the night.
Three days' rain will empty any sky.
A deep, clear sky of fleckless blue
Breeds storms within a day or two.
When the wind is in the east,
It's good for neither man nor beast.
When the wind is in the north,
The old folk should not venture forth,
When the wind is in the south,
It blows the bait in the fishes' mouth.
When the wind is in the west,
It is of all the winds the best.
An opening and a shetting
Is a sure sign of a wetting.

(Another version)
Open and shet,
Sure sign of wet.

(Still another)

Continued on next page

Continued from previous page

It's lighting up to see to rain.
Evening red and morning gray
Sends the traveler on his way.
Evening gray and morning red
Sends the traveler home to bed.
Red sky at morning, the shepherd takes warning;
Red sky at night is the shepherd's delight.
If the sun goes down cloudy Friday, sure of a clear Sunday.
Between eleven and two
You can tell what the weather is going to do.
Rain before seven, clear before eleven.
Fog in the morning, bright sunny day.
If it rains, and the sun is shining at the same time, the devil is
    whipping his wife and it will surely rain to-morrow.
If it clears off during the night, it will rain shortly again.
Sun drawing water, sure sign of rain.
A circle round the moon means "storm." As many stars as are in
    circle, so many days before it will rain.
Sudden heat brings thunder.
A storm that comes against the wind is always a thunderstorm.
The oak and the ash draw lightning. Under the birch the cedar,
    and balsam you are safe.
East wind brings rain.
West wind brings clear, bright, cool weather.
North wind brings cold.
South wind brings heat. (On Atlantic coast.)
The tree-frog cries before rain.
Swallows flying low is a sign of rain; high, of clearing weather.
The rain follows the wind, and the heavy blast is just before the
    shower.

NIGHT SKIES

THE STARS

Seen With the Naked Eye

Whether he expects to use them as guides or not, every boy should learn
the principal constellations and the important stars. A non-scientific friend

said to me once: "I am always glad that I learned the principal star groups when I was young. I have never forgotten them, and, no matter in what strange country I find myself, I can always look up at night, and see the old familiar stars that shone on me in my home in my own country."

THE DIPPER OR GREAT BEAR

Many American boys know the Dipper or Great Bear. This is, perhaps, the most important star group in our sky, because of its size, peculiar form, and the fact that it never sets in our latitude, and last, that it always points out the Pole-star, and, for this reason, it is sometimes known as the Pointers. It is called the Dipper because it is shaped like a dipper with a long, bent handle. Why it is called the Great Bear is not so easy to explain. The classical legend has it that the nymph Calisto, having violated her vow, was changed by Diana into a bear, which, after death, was immortalized in the sky by Zeus. Another suggestion is that the earliest astronomers, the Chaldeans, called these stars "the shining ones," and their word happened to be very like the Greek *arktos* (a bear). Another explanation (I do not know who is authority for either) is that vessels in olden days were named for animals, etc. They bore at the prow the carved effigy of the namesake, and if the *Great Bear*, for example, made several very happy voyages by setting out when a certain constellation was in the ascendant, that constellation might become known as the *Great Bear's* constellation. Certainly, there is nothing in its shape to justify the name. Very few of the constellations, indeed, are like the thing they are called after. Their names were usually given for some fanciful association with the namesake, rather than for resemblance to it.

THE POLE OR NORTH STAR

The Pole-star is really the most important of the stars in our sky; it marks the north at all times; it alone is fixed in the heavens: all the other stars seem to swing around it once in twenty-four hours. It is in the end of the Little Bear's tail. But the Pole-star, or Polaris, is not a very bright one, and it would be hard to identify but for the help of the Dipper, or Pointers.

The outside (Alpha and Beta) of the Dipper points nearly to Polaris, at a distance equal to three and one half times the space that separates these two stars of the Dipper's outer side.

Various Indian peoples call the Pole-star the "Home Star," and "The Star that Never Moves," and the Dipper they call the "Broken Back."

The last star but one in the Dipper, away from the pole—that is, the star at the bend of the handle, —is known to astronomers as Mizar, one of the Horses. Just above it, and tucked close in, is a smaller star known to astronomers as Alcor, or the Rider. The Indians call these two the "Old Squaw and the Pappoose on Her Back." In the old world, from very ancient times, these have been used as tests of eyesight. To be able to see Alcor with the naked eye means that one has excellent eyesight. So also on the plains, the old folks would ask the children at night, "Can you see the pappoose on the old squaw's back?" And when the youngster saw it, and proved that he did by a right description, they rejoiced that he had the eyesight which is the first requisite of a good hunter.

The Great Bear is also to be remembered as the Pointers for another reason. It is the hour-hand of the woodman's clock. It goes once around the North Star in about twenty-four hours, the same way as the sun, and for the same reason—that it is the earth that is going and leaving them behind.

The time in going around is not exactly twenty-four hours, so that the position of the Pointers varies with the seasons, but, as a rule, the bowl of the Dipper swings one and one half times the width of the opening (*i.e.*, fifteen degrees) in one hour. If it went a quarter of the circle, that would mean you had slept a quarter of a day, or six hours.

Each fifteen days the stars seem to be an hour earlier; in three months they gain one fourth of the circle, and in a year gain the whole circle.

ORION

Orion with its striking array of brilliant stars, Betelguese, Rigel, the Three Kings, etc., is generally admitted to be the finest constellation in the heavens.

Orion was the hunter giant who went to Heaven when he died, and now marches around the great dome, but is seen only in the winter, because, during the summer, he passes over during daytime. Thus he is still the hunter's constellation. The three stars of his belt are called the "Three Kings."

Sirius, the Great Dog-star, is in the head of Orion's hound, and following farther back is the Little Dog-star, Procyon.

In old charts of the stars, Orion is shown with his hound, hunting the bull, Taurus.

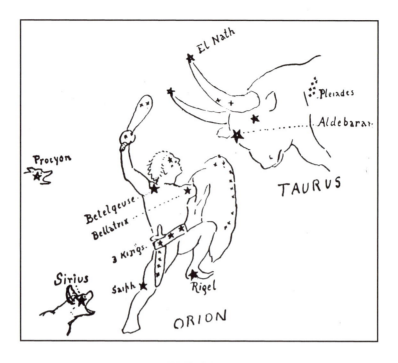

PLEIADES

Pleiades can be seen in winter as a cluster of small stars between Aldebaran and Algol, or, a line drawn from the back bottom through the front rim of the Dipper, about two Dipper lengths, touches this little group. They are not far from Aldebaran, being on the shoulder of the Bull, of which Aldebaran is the right eye. They may be considered the seven arrow wounds made by Orion. They are nearer the Pole-star than Aldebaran is, and on the side away from the Dipper; also, they are nearly on a line between Beta of the Dipper (front bottom) and Capella.

THE MOON

The moon is one fifth the diameter of the earth, about one fiftieth of the bulk and is about a quarter million miles away. Its course, while very irregular, is nearly the same as the apparent course of the sun. But "in winter the full moon is at an altitude in the sky near the limit attained by the sun in summer, ... and even, at certain times, five degrees higher. It is the contrary in summer, a season when the moon remains very low" (F.).

The moon goes around the earth in 27 1/4 days. It loses nearly three fourths of an hour each night; that is, it rises that much later.

HOW TO FIND YOUR WAY BY THE STARS

It is very important that those who frequent the forest should be sufficiently familiar with the stars to be able to tell their way by them. Often a compass is lost or damaged or there is not enough light to see the landmarks. At such a time a knowledge of how to find the Pole star is invaluable for, to the experienced woodsman, a glimpse of this star is equivalent to consulting a compass. It is really the most important of the stars we see, although not a very bright one, because it marks the North at all times and is fixed in its place, while all the other stars seem to swing around it once in each twenty-four hours, which makes it impracticable to use them for guidance. The Dipper or Great Bear is

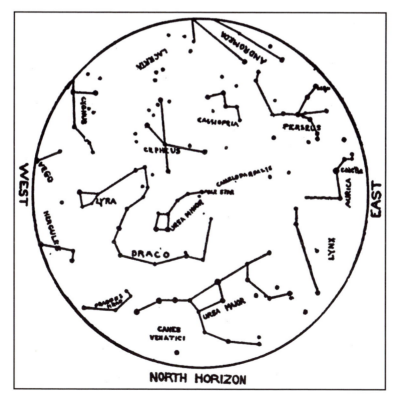

BIG DIPPER AND LITTLE DIPPER W/NORTH STAR

well known on account of the size, peculiar shape and brilliancy of this group, and the fact that it never sets in this latitude.

This group always points out the Pole star or Polaris, which is about in a line with the stars (Alpha and Beta) which form the outside of the Dipper at a distance about three and a half times as great as the space separating these two stars. This star always points out the North. If the imaginary line between Alpha and Beta and Polaris is continued about the same distance beyond Polaris it will meet Cassiopeia, five stars in the shape of a W, which, like the Great Bear, is always seen in our latitude. With these directions it should be always easy to locate Polaris.

SNAKE BITES TO BEE STINGS

Snakes are to the animal world what toadstools are to the vegetable world—wonderful things, beautiful things, but fearsome things, because some of them are deadly poison. But out of one hundred and eleven species of snakes found in the United States, only seventeen are

CORAL SNAKE

poisonous. They are found in every state, but are most abundant in the Southwest.

These may be divided into Coral Snakes, Moccasins, and Rattlers.

The Coral Snakes are found in the Southern States. They are very much like harmless snakes in shape, but are easily distinguished by their remarkable colors, "broad alternating rings of red and black, the latter bordered with very narrow rings of yellow."

The Rattlesnakes are readily told at once by the rattle.

But the Moccasins are not so easy. There are two kinds: the Water Moccasin, or Cotton-mouth, found in South Carolina, Georgia, Florida, Alabama, and Louisiana, and the Copperhead, which is the Highland, or Northern Moccasin or Pilot Snake, found from Massachusetts to Florida and west to Illinois and Texas.

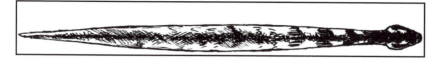

WATER MOCCASIN

Here are distinguishing marks: The Moccasins, as well as the Rattlers, have on each side of the head, between the eye and nostril, a deep pit.

The pupil of the eye is an upright line, as in a cat; the harmless snakes have a round pupil.

The Moccasins have a single row of plates under the tail, while the harmless snakes have a double row.

The Water Moccasin is dull olive with wide black transverse bands.

The Copperhead is dull hazel brown, marked across the back with dumb-bells of reddish brown; the top of the head more or less coppery.

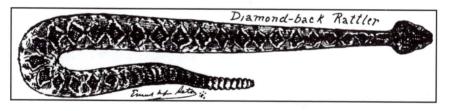

RATTLE SNAKE

Both Moccasins and Rattlers have a flat triangular head, which is much wider than the thin neck; while most harmless snakes have a narrow head that shades off into the neck.

Rattlesnakes are found generally distributed over the United States, southern Ontario, southern Alberta, and Saskatchewan.

HOW DOES A SNAKE BITE?

Remember, the tongue is a feeler, not a sting. The "stinging" is done by two long hollow teeth, or fangs, through which the poison is squirted into the wound.

The striking distance of a snake is about one third the creature's length, and the stroke is so swift that no creature can dodge it.

The snake can strike farthest and surest when it is ready coiled, but can strike a little way when travelling.

You cannot disarm a poisonous snake without killing it. If the fangs are removed others come quickly to take their place. In fact, a number of small, half-grown fangs are always waiting ready to be developed.

HARMLESS SNAKES

Far the greatest number of our snakes are harmless, beautiful, and beneficent. They are friendly to the farmer, because, although some destroy a few birds, chickens, ducklings, and game, the largest part of their food is mice and insects. The Blacksnake, the Milk Snake, and one or two others, will bite in self-defence, but they have no poison fangs, and the bite is much like the prick of a bramble.

There are no infallible rules for expedient identification of poisonous snakes in the field, because the guidelines all require close observation or manipulation of the snake's body. The best strategy is to leave all snakes alone.

REDUCE THE CHANCE OF ACCIDENTAL SNAKEBITE:

- Don't sleep next to brush, tall grass, large boulders, or trees. They provide hiding places for snakes. Place your sleeping bag in a clearing. Use mosquito netting tucked well under the bag. This netting should provide a good barrier.
- Don't put your hands into dark places, such as rock crevices, heavy brush, or hollow logs, without first investigating.
- Don't step over a fallen tree. Step on the log and look to see if there is a snake resting on the other side.
- Don't walk through heavy brush or tall grass without looking down. Look where you are walking.
- Don't pick up any snake unless you are absolutely positive it is not venomous.
- Don't pick up freshly killed snakes without first severing the head. The nervous system may still be active and a dead snake can deliver a bite.

Although venomous snakes use their venom to secure food, they also use it for self-defense. Human accidents occur when you don't see or hear the snake, when you step on them, or when you walk too close to them.

FIRST AID FOR SNAKEBITE & STINGS

BITES AND STINGS

Type	First aid
Snakebite	1. Get the casualty away from the snake. 2. Remove all rings and bracelets from the affected extremity. 3. Reassure the casualty and keep him quiet. 4. Apply constricting band(s) 1–2 finger widths proximal to the bite. One finger should be able to be slipped between the band and skin. ARM or LEG Bite—Place one band above and one band below the bite site. HAND or FOOT Bite—Place one band above the wrist or ankle. 5. Immobilize the affected limb in a position below the level of the heart. 6. Kill the snake, if possible, (without damaging its head or endangering yourself) and send it with the casualty. 7. Seek medical treatment immediately.
Brown Recluse Black Widow Spider bites	1. Keep the casualty calm. 2. Wash the area. 3. Apply ice or a freeze pack, if available. 4. Seek medical treatment.
Tarantula bite, Scorpion sting, Ant bites	1. Wash the area. 2. Apply ice or a freeze pack, if available.

...Continued

BITES AND STINGS *(Continued)*

Type	First aid
	3. Apply baking soda, calamine lotion, or meat tenderizer to the bite site to relieve pain and itching.
	4. If site of bite(s) or sting(s) is on the face, neck (possible airway blockage), or genital area, or if reaction is severe, or if the sting is by the dangerous Southwestern scorpion, keep the casualty as quiet as possible and seek immediate medical aid.
Bee stings	1. If the stinger is present, remove by scraping with a knife or finger nail. DO NOT squeeze venom sack on stinger, more venom may be injected.
	2. Wash the area.
	3. Apply ice or freeze pack, if available.
	4. If allergic signs or symptoms appear, be prepared to perform CPR and seek medical assistance.
Human and Other animal Bites	1. Cleanse the wound thoroughly with soap or detergent solution.
	2. Flush bite well with water.
	3. Cover bite with a sterile dressing.
	4. Immobilize injured extremity.
	5. Transport casualty to a medical treatment facility.
	6. Kill the animal, if possible, without damaging its head or endangering yourself, and send it with the casualty.

MEASURING DISTANCE IN THE FIELD

The height of a tree is easily measured when on a level, open place, by measuring the length of its shadow, then comparing that with your own shadow, or that of a ten-foot pole.

Thus, the ten-foot pole is casting a fifteen-foot shadow, and the tree's shadow is one hundred and fifty feet long, apply the simple rule of three.

$$15 : 150 :: 10 : x = 100$$

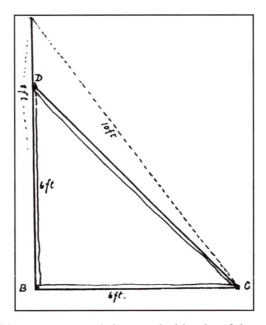

But it is seldom so easy, and the good old rule of the triangle can be safely counted on: Get a hundred or more feet from your tree, on open ground, as nearly as possible on the level of its base. Set up a ten-foot pole (*A B*). Then mark the spot where the exact line from the top of the tree over the top of the pole touches the ground (*C*). Now measure the distance from that spot (*C*) to the foot of the ten-foot pole (*B*); suppose it is twenty feet. Measure also the distance from that spot (*C*) to the base of the tree (*D*); suppose it is one hundred and twenty feet, then your problem is:

20 : 10 :: 120 : x = 60

i.e., if at that angle twenty feet from the eye gives ten feet elevation, one hundred and twenty feet must give sixty.

To make a right angle, make a triangle whose sides are exactly six, eight, and ten feet or inches each (or multiples of these). The angle opposite the ten must be a true right angle. There are many ways of measuring distance across rivers, etc., without crossing. The simplest, perhaps, is by the equilateral triangle. Cut three poles of exactly equal length; peg them together into a triangle. Lay this on the bank of the river so one side points to some point on the opposite bank. Drive in three pegs to mark the exact points of this triangle (*A,B,C*). Then move it along the bank until you find a place (*F,E,G*) where its base is on line with the two pegs, where the base used to be, and one side in line with the point across the river (D). The width of the river is seven eighths of the base of this great triangle.

ROCKS AND FOSSILS

Geologists study the materials of the earth's crust, the processes continually changing its surface, and the forms and structures thus produced. In a day's tramp one may see much under each of these heads.

The earth's crust is made up chiefly of hard rocks, which outcrop in many places, but are largely covered by thin, loose, surface materials. Rocks may be igneous, which have cooled from a melted condition; or sedimentary, which are made of layers spread one upon another by water currents or waves, or by winds.

Igneous rocks, while still molten, have been forced into other rocks from below, or poured out on the surface from volcanoes. They are chiefly made of crystals of various minerals, such as quartz, felspar, mica, and pyrite. Granite often contains large crystals of felspar or mica. Some igneous rocks, especially lavas, are glassy; others are so fine grained that the crystals cannot be seen.

In places one may find veins filling cracks in the rocks, and made of material deposited from solution in water. Many valuable minerals and ores occur in such veins, and fine specimens can sometimes be obtained from them.

Sedimentary rock is formed of material usually derived from the breaking up and wearing away of older rocks. When first deposited, the materials are loose, but later, when covered by other beds, they become hardened into solid rock. If the layers were of sand, the rock is sandstone; if of clay, it is shale. Rocks made of layers of pebbles are called conglomerate or pudding-stone; those of limy material, derived perhaps from shells, are limestone. Many sedimentary rocks contain fossils, which are the shells or bones of animals or the stems and leaves of plants living in former times, and buried by successive beds of sand or mud spread over them. Much of the land is covered by a thin surface deposit of clay, sand, or gravel, which is yet loose material and which shows the mode of formation of sedimentary rocks.

Some rocks have undergone, since their formation, great pressure or heat and have been much changed. They are called metamorphic rocks.

Some are now made of crystals though at first they were not; in others the minerals have become arranged in layers closely resembling the beds of sedimentary rocks; still others, like slate, tend to split into thin plates.

The earth's surface is continually being changed; the outcropping hard rock is worn away by wind and rain, and is broken up by frost, by solution of some minerals, etc. The loose material formed is blown away or washed away by rain and deposited elsewhere by streams in gravel bars, sand beds, and mud flats. The streams cut away their beds, aided by the sand and pebbles washed along. Thus the hills are being worn down and the valleys deepened and widened, and the materials of the land are slowly being moved toward the sea, again to be deposited in beds.

Along the coast the waves, with the pebbles washed about, are wearing away the land and spreading out its materials in new beds elsewhere. The shore is being cut back in some places and built out in others. Rivers bring down sand and mud and build deltas or bars at their mouths.

Volcanoes pour out melted rock on the surface, and much fine material is blown out in eruptions. Swamps are filled by dead vegetable matter and by sand and mud washed in. These materials form new rocks and build up the surface. Thus the two processes, the wearing down in some places and the building up in others, are tending to bring the surface to a uniform level. Another process, so slow that it can be observed only through long periods of time, tends to deform the earth's crust and to make the surface more irregular. In times past, layers of rock once horizontal have been bent and folded into great arches and troughs, and large areas of the earth's surface have been raised high above sea-level.

At almost any rock outcrop the result of the breaking-up process may be seen; the outer portion is softer, more easily broken, and of different color from the fresh rock, as shown by breaking open a large piece. The wearing away of the land surface is well shown in rain gullies, and the carrying along and depositing of sand and gravel may be seen in almost any stream. In the Northern states and Canada, which at one time were covered by a great sheet of ice, moving southward and grinding off the surface over which it passed, most of the rock outcrops are smoothly rounded and many show scratches made by pebbles dragged along by the ice. The hills too have smoother and rounder outlines, as compared with those farther south where the land has been carved only by rain and streams. Along the coast the wearing away of the land by waves is shown at cliffs, found where the coast is high, and by the abundant pebbles on the beaches, which are built of material torn from the land by the waves. Sand bars and tidal flats show the deposition of material brought by streams and spread out by currents. Sand dunes and barrens illustrate the carrying and spreading out of fine material by the wind.

In many regions the beds of sedimentary rocks, which must have been nearly horizontal when formed, are now found sloping at various angles or standing on edge, the result of slow deforming of these beds at an earlier time. As some beds are more easily worn away than others, the hills and valleys in such regions owe their form and position largely to the different extent to which the harder and softer beds have been worn down by weather and by streams. The irregular line of many coasts is likewise due to the different hardness of the rocks along the shore.

It is by the study of the rocks and of the remains of life found in them, by observing the way in which the surface of the earth is being

FOSSIL HUNTER'S KIT

Map
Compass
Long Tape Measure
Pocket Lens (magnifying-glass)
Notebook
Pencil and Pen
Camera
Hardhat
Goggles or Safety Glasses
Gloves
Trowel
Mallet
Geological Hammer
Chisels (guarded)
Small Brush
Large Brush
Spade
Plastic Sieve
Plaster Bandages (for setting or jacketing fragile fossils)
Dental Picks

changed and examining the results of those changes and by concluding that similar results were produced in former times in the same way,
that geologists are able to read much of the past history of the earth,
uncounted years before there were men upon it.

STANDARD METRIC WEIGHTS & MEASURES

The following cylinders give measure of liquid volumes in common use:

	Dia. in.	Height in.
1 gill (7.2 cu. in.)	1 3/4	3
1/2 pint	2 1/4	3 5/8
1 pint	3 1/2	3
1 quart	3 1/2	6
1 gallon	7	6
2 gallon	7	12
8 gallon	14	12
10 gallon	14	15

DRY MEASURE

2 pints = 1 quart
4 quarts = 1 gallon = 8 pints
2 gallons = 1 peck = 16 pints = 8 gallons
4 peeks = 1 bushel (struck) = 64 pints = 32
quarts = 8 gallons

SHORT METRIC TABLES

The common units in the metric tables of measurements can be classed
as follows for simplicity:

LENGTH

10 millimeters = 1 centimeter.
100 centimeters = 1 meter = 39.36982 inches.
1000 meters = 1 kilometer.

VOLUME

1000 cubic centimeters = 1 liter = 1.05671 quarts U. S.
1000 liters = 1 cubic meter.
1 centimeter of water at 4° centigrade weighs 1 gram.
1 liter of water at 4° centigrade weighs 1 kilogram.

WEIGHT

1000 milligrams = 1 gram.
1000 grams = 1 kilogram.
1000 kilograms = 1 metric ton = 2204.6 lbs. avoirdupois.

AREA

10,000 square centimeters = 1 square meter.
100 square meters = 1 are.
100 ares = 1 hectare.
100 hectares = 1 square kilometer.

METRIC CONVERSION TABLE OF WEIGHTS

1 grain = 0.0647989 grams
1 ounce, avoirdupois = 28.3496 grams
1 ounce, troy = 31.10348 grams
1 ton, 2000 pounds = 907.186 kilograms
1 ton, 2240 pounds = 1.016 metric tons
1 gram = 15.432 grains
1 kilogram = 2.2046 pounds
1 tonne or metric ton = 2204.6 pounds

METRIC CONVERSION TABLE OF LENGTHS

1 inch = 2.54 centimeters
1 foot = 0.3048 meter
1 yard = 0.914402 meter.
1 mile = 1.60935 kilometers
1 millimeter = 0.03937 inch

1 centimeter = 0.3937 inch
1 meter = 39.37 inches
1 kilometer = 3280.83 feet = 0.62137 mile

METRIC CONVERSION TABLE OF VOLUME

1 cubic inch = 16.387 cubic centimeters
1 cubic foot = 0.02832 cubic meter = 28.317 liters
1 cubic yard = 0.7645 cubic meter
1 U. S. gallon = 3.78543 liters
1 bushel = 0.35242 hectoliter
1 perch = 0.700846 cubic meter
1 cubic centimeter = 0.0610234 cubic inch
1 cubic meter = 35.314 cubic feet = 1.308 cubic yards
1 liter = 0.26417 U. S. gallon = 61.023 cubic inches
1 hectoliter = 2.8375 bushels

METRIC CONVERSION TABLE OF SURFACE

1 square inch = 6.45163 square centimeters
1 square foot = 0.0929034 square meter
1 square yard = 0.836131 square meter
1 acre = 4046.87 square meters
1 square mile = 2.59000 square kilometers
1 square centimeter = 0.15500 square inch
1 square meter = 10.764 square feet
1 hectare = 2.47104 acres = 107,641 square feet
1 square kilometer = 0.386101 square mile

PROPERTIES OF THE CIRCLE

Diameter × 3.14159 = circumference
Diameter × 0.8862 = side of an equal square
Diameter × 0.7071 = side of an inscribed square
Diameter^2 × 0.7854 = area of a circle
Radius × 6.28318 = circumference
Circumference + 3.14159 = diameter

1. The circle contains a greater area than any plane figure, bounded by an equal perimeter or outline.
2. The areas of circles are to each other as the squares of their diameters. Any circle whose diameter is double that of another contains four times the area of the other.
3. Area of a circle is equal to the area of a triangle whose base equals the circumference, and perpendicular equals the radius.

SURVIVAL

MOTTO FROM THE *U.S. ARMY RANGER HANDBOOK*

With training, equipment, and the WILL TO SURVIVE, you will find you can overcome any obstacle you may face. You will survive. You must understand the emotional states associated with survival; "knowing thyself" is extremely important in a survival situation. It bears directly on how well you cope with serious stresses, anxiety, pain, injury, illness; cold, heat, thirst, hunger, fatigue, sleep deprivation, boredom, loneliness and isolation.

You can overcome and reduce the shock of being isolated behind enemy lines if you keep the key word S-U-R-V-I-V-A-L foremost in your mind. Its letters can help guide you in your actions.

S - Size up the situation; size up your surroundings; size up your physical condition; size up your equipment.

U - Undue haste makes waste; don't be too eager to move. Plan your moves.

R - Remember where you are in relation to: the location of enemy units and controlled areas; The location of friendly units and controlled areas; The location of local water sources (this is especially important in the desert); Areas that will provide good cover and concealment. The above information will allow you to make intelligent decisions when you are in a survival/evasion situation.

V - Vanquish fear and panic.

I - Improvise; the situation can be improved. Learn to use natural things around you for different needs. Use your imagination.

V - Value living. Remember your goal - getting out alive. Stubbornness, a refusal to give into problems and obstacles that face you, will give you the mental and physical strength to endure.

A - Act like the natives; watch their daily routines. When, where, and how they get their food. Where they get their water.

L - Live by your wits. Learn basic skills.

BASICS OF SURVIVAL

WATER. Water is one of your most urgent needs in a survival situation. You can't live long without it, especially in hot areas where you lose so much through sweating. Even in cold areas, you need a minimum of

2 quarts of water a day to maintain efficiency. More than three-fourths of your body is composed of fluids. Your body loses fluid as a result of heat, cold, stress, and exertion. The fluid your body loses must be replaced for you to function effectively. So, one of your first objectives is to obtain an adequate supply of water.

Purification. Purify all water before drinking, either

1. by boiling for at least one minute (plus 1 minute for each additional 1,000 feet above sea level) or boil for 10 minutes no matter where you are;
2. by using water purification tablets or
3. by adding 8 drops of 2 1/2% solution of iodine to a quart (canteen full) of water and letting it stand for 10 minutes before drinking. Rain water collected directly in clean containers or on plants is generally safe to drink without purifying. Don't drink urine or sea water—the salt content is too high—Old bluish sea ice can be used, but new, gray ice may be salty. Glacier ice is safe to melt and drink.

Desert Environment. There are four indicators or signs of water that you should look for in the desert. They are: animal trails, vegetation, birds, and civilization.

Survival Water Still. For the below ground still you will need a digging tool.

You should select a site where you believe the soil will contain moisture (such as a dry stream bed or a spot where rain water has collected), where the soil is easy to dig, and where sunlight hits most of the day. Proceed as follows:

Dig a bowl-shaped hole approximately 3 feet across and 2 feet deep.

Dig a sump in center of the hole. The depth and the perimeter of the sump will depend on the size of the container that you have to set in it. The bottom of the sump should allow the container to stand upright.

Anchor the tubing to the bottom of the container by forming a loose overhand knot in the tubing.

Place the container upright in the sump.

Extend the unanchored end of the tubing up, over, and beyond the lip of the hole.

Place plastic sheeting over the hole covering the edge with soil to hold it in place.

Place a rock in the center of the plastic.

Allow the plastic to lower into the hole until it is about 15 inches below ground level. The plastic now forms an inverted cone with the rock at its apex. Make sure that the apex of the cone is directly over your container. Also make sure the plastic cone does not touch the sides of the hole because the earth will absorb the condensed water.

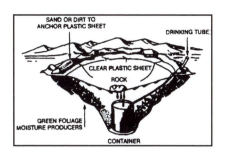

SURVIVAL WATER STILL

Put more soil on the edges of the plastic to hold it securely in place and to prevent loss of moisture.

Plug the tube when not being used so that moisture will not evaporate.

You can drink water without disturbing the still by using the tube as a straw. You may want to use plants in the hole as a moisture source. If so, when you dig the hole you should dig out additional soil from the sides of the hole to form a slope on which to place the plants. Then proceed as above.

PLANT FOOD

There are many plants throughout the world. Tasting or swallowing even a small portion of some can cause severe discomfort, extreme internal disorders, or death. Therefore, if you have the slightest doubt as to the edibility of a plant, apply the universal edibility test described below before eating any part of it.

Universal Edibility Test. Before testing a plant for edibility, make sure there are a sufficient number of plants to make testing worth your time and effort. You need more than 24 hours to apply the edibility test outlined below:

1. Test only one part of a potential food plant at a time.
2. Break the plant into its basic components, leaves, stems, roots, buds, and flowers.
3. Smell the food for strong or acid odors. Keep in mind that smell alone does not indicate a plant is edible.
4. Do not eat for 8 hours before starting the test.

5. During the 8 hours you are abstaining from eating, test for contact poisoning by placing a piece of the plant you are testing on the inside of your elbow or wrist. Usually 15 minutes is enough time to allow for reaction.
6. During the test period, take nothing by mouth except purified water and the plant part being tested.
7. Select a small portion and prepare it the way you plan to eat it.
8. Before putting the prepared plant part in your mouth, touch a small portion (a pinch) to the outer surface of the lip to test for burning or itching.
9. If after 3 minutes there is no reaction on your lip, place the plant part on your tongue, holding there for 15 minutes.
10. If there is no reaction, thoroughly chew a pinch and hold it in your mouth for 15 minutes. DO NOT SWALLOW.
11. If no burning, itching, numbing, stinging, or other irritation occurs during the 15 minutes, swallow the food.
12. Wait 8 hours. If any ill effects occur during this period, induce vomiting and drink a lot of water.
13. If no ill effects occur eat 1/2 cup of the same plant part prepared the same way. Wait another 8 hours. If no ill effects occur, the plant part as prepared is safe for eating.

DO NOT eat unknown plants that have the below characteristics:
Have a milky sap or a sap that turns black when exposed to air;
Are mushroom like; Resemble onion or garlic; Resemble parsley, parsnip, or dill; Have carrot-like leaves, roots, or tubers;

Your survival kit need not be elaborate. You need only functional items that will meet your needs and case to hold the items. For the case, you might want to use a Band-Aid box, a first aid case, an ammunitio pouch, or another suitable case. This case should be—

- Water repellent or waterproof
- Easy to carry or attach to your body
- Suitable to accept varisized components
- Durable

COLD CLIMATE KIT

- Food packets
- Snare wire
- Smoke, illumination signals
- Waterproof match box
- Saw/knife blade
- Wood matches
- First aid kit
- MC-1 magnetic compass
- Pocket knife
- Saw-knife-shovel handle
- Frying pan
- Illuminating candles
- Compressed trioxane fuel
- Signaling mirror
- Survival fishing kit
- Plastic spoon
- Survival Manual (AFM 64–5)
- Poncho
- Insect headnet
- Ejector snap
- Attaching strap
- Kit, outer case
- Kit, inner case
- Shovel
- Water bag
- Packing list
- Sleeping bag

HOT CLIMATE KIT

- Canned drinking water
- Waterproof matchbox
- Plastic whistle
- Smoke, illumination signals
- Pocket knife
- Signaling mirror
- Plastic water bag
- First aid kit
- Sunblock
- Plastic spoon
- Food packets
- Compressed trioxane fuel
- Fishing tackle kit
- Ejector snap
- Snare wire
- Frying pan
- Wood matches
- Insect headnet
- Reversible sun hat
- Tool kit
- Kit, packing list
- Tarpaulin
- Kit, inner case
- Kit, outer case
- Attaching strap
- MC-1 magnetic compass

FIELD-EXPEDIENT DIRECTION FINDING

USING THE SUN AND SHADOWS

The earth's relationship to the sun can help you to determine direction on earth. The sun always rises in the east and sets in the west, but not exactly due east or due west. There is also some seasonal variation. In the southern hemisphere, the sun will be due south when at its highest point in the sky, or when an object casts no appreciable shadow. In the southern hemisphere, this same noonday sun will mark due north. In the northern hemisphere, shadows will move clockwise. Shadows will move counterclockwise in the southern hemisphere. With practice, you can use shadows to determine both direction and time of day. The shadow methods used for direction finding are the shadow-tip and watch methods.

Shadow-Tip Methods. In the first shadow-tip method, find a straight stick 1 meter long, and a level spot free of brush on which the stick will cast a definite shadow. This method is simple and accurate and consists of four steps:

Step 1. Place the stick or branch into the ground at a level spot where it will cast a distinctive shadow. Mark the shadow's tip with a stone, twig, or other means. This first shadow mark is always west—everywhere on earth.

Step 2. Wait 10 to 15 minutes until the shadow tip moves a few centimeters. Mark the shadow tip's new position in the same way as the first.

Step 3. Draw a straight line through the two marks to obtain an approximate east-west line.

Step 4. Stand with the first mark (west) to your left and the second mark to your right—you are now facing north. This fact is true everywhere on earth.

An alternate method is more accurate but requires more time. Set up your shadow stick and mark the shadow in the morning. Use a piece of string to draw a clean arc through this mark and around the stick. At midday, the shadow will shrink and disappear. In the afternoon, it will lengthen again and at the point where it touches the arc, make a second mark. Draw a line through the two marks to get an accurate east-west line.

The Watch Method. You can determine direction using a common or analog watch—one that has hands. The direction will be accurate

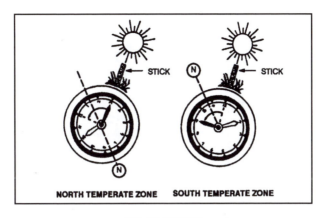

WATCH METHOD

if you are using true local time, without any changes for daylight-saving time. Remember, the further you are from the equator, the more accurate this method will be. If you have a digital watch, you can overcome this obstacle. Quickly draw a watch on a circle of paper with the correct time on it and use it to determine your direction at that time.

In the northern hemisphere, hold the watch horizontal and point the hour hand at the sun. Bisect the angle between the hour hand and the 12 o'clock mark to get the north-south line. If there is any doubt as to which end of the line is north, remember that the sun rises in the east, sets in the west, and is due south at noon. The sun is in the east before noon and in the west after noon.

Note: If your watch is set on daylight savings time, use the midway point between the hour hand and 1 o'clock to determine the north-south line.

In the southern hemisphere, point the watch's 12 o'clock mark toward the sun and a midpoint halfway between 12 and the hour hand will give you the north-south line.

USING THE MOON

Because the moon has no light of its own, we can only see it when it reflects the sun's light. As it orbits the earth on its 28-day circuit, the

1 Mark the shadow's tip.

2 Mark the new position and draw a line through the two marks.

3 Stand with the first mark to your left and the second mark to your right—you are now facing north.

SHADOW–TIP METHOD

shape of the reflected light varies according to its position. We say there is a new moon or no moon when it is on the opposite side of the earth from the sun. Then, as it moves away from the earth's shadow, it begins to reflect light from its right side and waxes to become a full moon before waning, or losing shape, to appear as a sliver on the left side. You can use this information to identify direction.

If the moon rises before the sun has set, the illuminated side will be the west. If the moon rises after midnight, the illuminated side will be the east. This obvious discovery provides us with a rough east-west reference during the night.

OTHER MEANS OF DETERMINING DIRECTION

The old saying about using moss on a tree to indicate north is not accurate because moss grows completely around some trees. Actually, growth is more lush on the side of the tree facing the south in the Northern Hemisphere and vice versa in the Southern Hemisphere. If there are several felled trees around for comparison, look at the stumps. Growth is more vigorous on the side toward the equator and the tree growth rings will be more widely spaced. On the other hand, the tree growth rings will be closer together on the side toward the poles.

Wind direction may be helpful in some instances where there are prevailing directions and you know what they are.

Recognizing the differences between vegetation and moisture patterns on north- and south-facing slopes can aid in determining direction. In the northern hemisphere, north-facing slopes receive less sun than south-facing slopes and are therefore cooler and damper. In the summer, north-facing slopes retain patches of snow. In the winter, the trees and open areas on south-facing slopes are the first to lose their snow, and ground snow pack is shallower.

HAND MADE ARMS

In survival situations, you may have to fashion any number and type of field-expedient tools and equipment to survive. Examples of tools and equipment that could make your life much easier are ropes, rucksacks, clothes, nets, and so on.

Weapons serve a dual purpose. You use them to obtain and prepare food and to provide self-defense. A weapon can also give you a feeling of security and provide you with the ability to hunt on the move.

CLUBS

You hold clubs, you do not throw them. As a field-expedient weapon, the club does not protect you. It can, however, extend your area of defense beyond your fingertips. It also serves to increase the force of a blow without injuring yourself. There are three basic types of clubs. They are the simple, weighted, and sling club.

Simple Club. A simple club is a staff or branch. It must be short enough for you to swing easily, but long enough and strong enough for you to damage whatever you hit. Its diameter should fit comfortably in your palm, but it should not be so thin as to allow the club to break easily upon impact. A straight-grained hardwood is best if you can find it.

Weighted Club. A weighted club is any simple club with a weight on one end. The weight may be a natural weight, such as a knot on the wood, or something added, such as a stone lashed to the club.

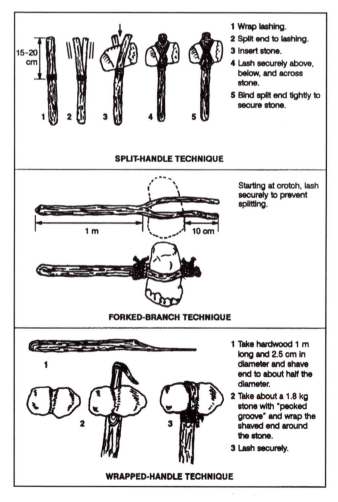

LASHING CLUBS

OTHER EXPEDIENT WEAPONS

You can make other field-expedient weapons such as the throwing stick, archery equipment, and the bola.

Throwing Stick. The throwing stick, commonly known as the rabbit stick, is very effective against small game (squirrels, chipmunks, and rabbits). The rabbit stick itself is a blunt stick, naturally curved at about a 45-degree angle. Select a stick with the desired angle from heavy hardwood such as oak. Shave off two opposite sides so that the stick

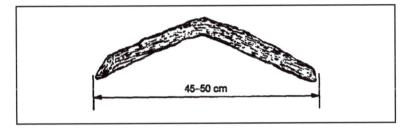

THROWING STICK

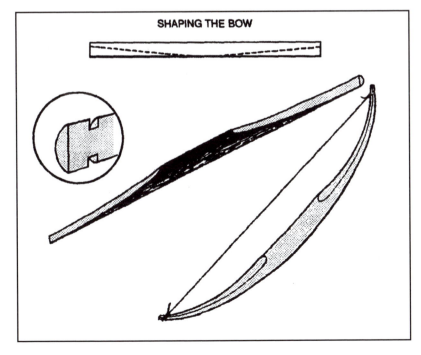

ARCHERY EQUIPMENT

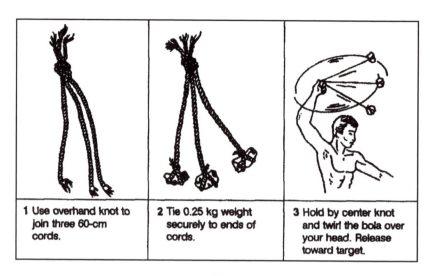

| 1 Use overhand knot to join three 60-cm cords. | 2 Tie 0.25 kg weight securely to ends of cords. | 3 Hold by center knot and twirl the bola over your head. Release toward target. |

BOLA

is flat like a boomerang. You must practice the throwing technique for accuracy and speed. First, align the target by extending the nonthrowing arm in line with the mid to lower section of the target. Slowly and repeatedly raise the throwing arm up and back until the throwing stick crosses the back at about a 45-degree angle or is in line with the non-throwing hip. Bring the throwing arm forward until it is just slightly above and parallel to the nonthrowing arm. This will be the throwing stick's release point. Practice slowly and repeatedly to attain accuracy.

Archery Equipment. You can make a bow and arrow from materials available in your survival area. While it may be relatively simple to make a bow and arrow, it is not easy to use one. You must practice using it a long time to be reasonably sure that you will hit your target. Also, a field-expedient bow will not last very long before you have to make a new one. For the time and effort involved, you may well decide to use another type of field-expedient weapon.

Bola. The bola is another field-expedient weapon that is easy to make. It is especially effective for capturing running game or low-flying fowl in a flock. To use the bola, hold it by the center knot and twirl it above your head. Release the knot so that the bola flies toward your target. When you release the bola, the weighted cords will separate. These cords will wrap around and immobilize the fowl or animal that you hit.

DEFENSIVE FIGHTING SKILLS

DEFENSIVE FIGHTING SKILLS

DEFENSE AGAINST A FRONTAL CHOKE

There are many ways to escape a choke hold. The trick is first to focus on getting the attacker to release his grip in your neck, windpipe or throat. Panic is likely to set in once your breathing is hindered, so a quick move is key.

Break your attacker's grip by swinging your arm up and back as if to throw a ball. This will knock his arm away, breaking his grip on you.

or

Raise your arm straight up, pressing your upper arm against your ear, and trapping your attacker's hand against your neck, then rotate away from him, also breaking his grip. With a quick, explosive motion, bring your arm down and push his arms away.

or

Reach in and grab your attacker's thumbs firmly and swing them downward and outward. Step back and pull his hands outward. You are now in control.

or

Keeping your elbows tight to your stomach, reach in and lock his thumbs in your hands and bring them in a straight downward motion. This will bring your attacker to his knees.

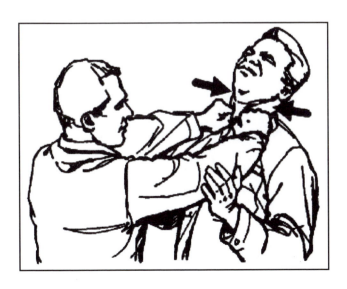

DEFENSE AGAINST HEADLOCK

The headlock is among the most common ways an attacker seeks to control his victim.

Spread your legs to allow yourself a better balance. Raise your arm that is closest your attacker and grab his hair from behind. Pull him steadily backward, tripping him over your extended leg, and bring him to the ground.

or

Instead of grabbing his hair, bring the same hand as above and grab his chin, pull him backward over your extended leg and bring him down.

DEFENSE AGAINST A REAR BEAR HUG

In this you defend against an attack from behind. The trick is to be aware of what is going on around you.

As you feel your attacker make his move, take a wider stance, and raise your arms from your shoulders, blocking him with your forearms. Then step out, turn and confront him.

DEFENSE AGAINST A ONE-ARMED ATTACK FROM BEHIND

In this attack from behind, instead of a bear hug with two arms, the attacker puts one arm around your neck, and puts his other hand on your arm. This is a very common rear attack, and is more dangerous than a bear hug because the arm around your neck is a choke hold.

Your first move is to firmly grab the wrist of his arm that is around your neck and pull it downward. Now he's no longer chocking you.

Widen your stance and lower your balance. Arch yourself forward and put all you weight onto the wrist you are holding and with an explosive movement, pull him forward and throw him to the ground.

or

Turn in towards his body and bring your leg that is closest to him behind his body and throwing your weight back against him, trip him and bring him down.

There is likely a moment in either of these two defenses when your attacker has let go of your free arm. This is a good opportunity for you to deliver him a sharp poke in the stomach with your elbow. But be careful or you may hurt him, and you wouldn't want to do that. Would you?

CLASSIC BASEBALL

CLASSIC BASEBALL

The number of *players* is usually nine.

Going to bat means that all the members of one side take their turn in regular order one after the other at batting, while all the members of the other side play in the field, on bases, pitch and catch. The team in the field tries to put out the team at bat.

Baseball is scored by *innings*. There are two halves in each inning—one for each team. A half lasts until three members of one team are put out; an inning lasts until three members of both teams are put out. There are nine innings in a game unless it is a tie, or otherwise changed by agreement of both teams.

Baseball is scored by *runs*. A run is when a batter succeeds in going around all three bases and home and is not put out before the third out is called.

Overrunning a base is when a base-runner goes beyond the bag and no part of his body touches it.

The *foul line* is back of the base line from home to first and from home to third—all the space on the other side is the field.

A *fair ball* is one which is over any portion of the home plate between the knee and shoulder of the batter. Such a ball is called a "strike," whether hit by the batter or not.

A *"ball"* is called by the umpire when a pitched ball does not go over any part of the plate or is below the knee or higher than the shoulder, and is not struck at by the batter. When the batter bats at such a ball, no matter how badly thrown, it counts as a strike. When four balls have been thrown before three strikes are called, the batter is given a base, that is, allowed to go to first without being put out.

A *strike* is

1. when any ball is batted at;
2. when it is a fair ball and not batted at;
3. a foul tip caught; and
4. a good ball interfered with by the batter.

A *foul tip* occurs when a ball is hit and the bat knocks it back of the foul line, no higher than the batter's bead. Such a ball, if caught, counts as a "strike."

A *foul ball* is one striking back of the foul line, higher than the head and not caught. Where a ball *hits* first and not where it *rolls* is the test of a foul.

A *foul strike* occurs when a ball is hit, and any part of the person of the batter is outside his box.

A *fair hit* is one which goes into the field.

A *bunt* is a ball struck soft, so as to fall near the home plate.

A *fly* is a ball batted high enough in the air to be caught before touching the ground. A grounder is one which skims along close to the ground.

An *illegal ball* is one pitched when any part of the pitcher's body is out of the box; or when he fails to heel the line; or when he takes more than one step forward. Any one of these mistakes entitles the batter or base-runner to a base.

A *balk* occurs when the pitcher makes a motion to deliver the ball and does not do it; or holds the ball too long and delays the game.

A *dead ball* is caused by a pitched ball hitting the batter, but does not entitle the batter to a base. If it is the third strike, the batter is out.

A *one-base* hit is one which enables the batter to get to first; *two-base hit*, or "two bagger," one which enables him to get second; and *three-base hit*, to third *without stopping. A home run* is made when the runner goes all the way round without stopping. An umpire calls "out" when the batter is to retire; and "safe" if he has reached the base before the ball or has not been tagged, or slides with the bag and clings to it.

A *double out* occurs when the ball reaches first base before the batter and then is thrown to second base before the base-runner from first gets there. In this way two are put out. This may occur on any base.

A *forced run* is where a base-runner holds a base and is forced on to the next base to make room for another base-runner or batter.

A *sacrifice hit* occurs when the batter hits the ball so that he will be put out, thus enabling a base-runner who is on third or second to score. While he is being put out at first, it may be quite easy for a runner to get home.

The ball is not in play, *i.e.*, no one can run or score,

1. when there is a foul strike;
2. when there is a foul hit ball not legally caught;
3. when there is a dead ball; and
4. when the base-runner is put out by being hit by the ball. In these cases the ball is in play again only when it is held by the pitcher in the box.

Rules for the Batter.—The batter is out:

1. If a third strike is caught by the catcher.
2. If there is a base-runner on first, the batter is out on a third strike whether it is caught or not; except when two are already out.
3. If the ball is not caught by the catcher, but is thrown to first base and is held by the first baseman while some part of his body touches the base—before the batter gets there.
4. If, as a base-runner, he is touched with the ball in the hands of a fielder before he reaches a base.
5. If he bats out of his her turn and makes a fair hit before it is discovered. The order of batting is made up before the game begins, and must then be adhered to.
6. If he fails to take his position within one minute when it is his turn to bat.

7. If a foul tip or a fair hit is caught.
8. If he makes a foul strike, *i.e.*, bats while any part of his body is outside the batter's box.
9. If he interferes with the catcher or intentionally fouls the ball.
10. If he intentionally gets in the way of a pitched ball.
11. If he is hit by the ball on the third strike, *i.e.*, intentionally fouls the ball and it hits him.

Rules for Base-Runners.—A base-runner can leave his base only when the ball has left the pitcher's hand and reached or missed the catcher. If he leaves at any other time he may be put out or called back. A base-runner who, at any time after he overruns first, is off base, may be put out if he is touched with the ball in the hands of a player. Only one base may be taken when a ball passes the batter or is fumbled, except when it is the third strike or four balls, then he takes all he can get.

A base-runner may take one base under the following conditions:

1. Immediately when the umpire calls four balls he goes to first.
2. If the pitcher does not give him time to return.
3. When a fair hit ball strikes the umpire.
4. If he is stopped or obstructed by an adversary.

When a fair or foul ball is caught the base-runner can only advance from the base *after the ball is caught*. If he starts before he must go back and touch base, or if touched with the ball before returning to the base, he is out. On a fair hit ball a base-runner runs all the bases he can get. A base-runner must be on base when the pitcher is ready to deliver the ball.

The base-runner must return to his base under the following conditions:

1. When there is a foul hit not legally caught. (When it is caught it is a strike and the base-runner can advance.)
2. When there is a foul strike.
3. When a dead ball is called.
4. When the umpire is struck by a ball thrown to the baseman.
5. When he leaves his base too soon.

The base-runner may be put out under the following conditions:

1. If a foul hit or fair hit is caught.
2. If the third strike is caught.
3. If he interferes with ball, for example kicking it.
4. If after three strikes or fair hits he is touched with the ball in the hands of a player, or the ball reaches the first base before he does.
5. If he runs more than three feet either side of the base line.
6. If he fails to avoid a fielder trying to field a batted ball, or obstructs a fielder.
7. If at any time, except when he overruns first, he is touched with the ball in the hands of a fielder when no part of his body touches the base, except when he goes back on a foul, or is ordered back by the umpire or given a base. If a base-runner overruns first and goes on to second, then he is not entitled to exemption for overrunning.
8. When a foul hit or fair hit is caught, not only is the batter out, but the base-runner also if the ball reaches the baseman before he returns to the base and touches it *after the ball was caught.*
9. When a hit ball strikes a base-runner, who is running between the bases.
10. If he fails to touch bases as he runs and the ball is returned first to the base that he did not touch.

A baseman on first need not touch the batter running to first; on a double play where a fair hit or foul hit is caught, the ball need only be held by the baseman. At all other times he must be tagged.

Test your baseball savvy by answering the following:

1. If there is a base-runner on first and on second and a grounder is hit to third, what will the third baseman do with the ball?
2. If there is a base-runner on second and the shortstop gets the ball, where will he throw it?
3. If there are base-runners on first and on second and the right fielder catches a fly, where will he throw it?
4. If there is a base-runner on third and the ball is hit to the second baseman, what does he do with it?
5. If there is a base-runner on third and the ball is bunted, and the catcher gets it, what will he do with it?

6. If all the bases are full and the ball is batted to the pitcher, what does he do with it?

7. If a hit grounder misses the pitcher and goes three feet one side of second base, what should the second baseman and pitcher do?

8. If there is a base-runner on third and the umpire calls four balls, where should the catcher throw the ball?

9. If all the bases are full and the umpire calls three strikes and the ball is caught, where should the catcher throw it?

10. If a pitched ball is missed by the catcher and he runs for it, what does the shortstop do?

11. When a base-runner has started from second and the ball gets to third before he does, who plays and where?

12. If there are base-runners on first and on second and the third strike is caught, where is the ball to be thrown?

13. If there is a base-runner on first and a hot grounder comes to the second baseman, where will he throw it?

14. If there is one out and base-runners on first and third and the third strike goes over the catcher's head, to whom is the ball thrown?

15. If there is a base-runner on each base and a grounder goes to the third baseman, what does he do with it? If it is a fly caught by him, what does he do?

16. When no base-runner is on bases and a hard single grounder goes out to the left field, where should the ball be returned?

17. When there is a base-runner on third and a single goes to the right fielder uncaught, where should it be returned?

18. When there is a base-runner on first and a grounder gets to first before the batter, what should the baseman do with the ball?

MORE THINGS THE ADVENTUROUS
BOY SHOULD KNOW

SIGN LANGUAGE

By Ernest Thompson Seton

Do You know Sign Language?

If not, do you realize that the Sign Language is an established mode of communication in all parts of the world.

Do you know that it is as old as the hills and is largely used in all public schools? And yet when I ask boys this question, "Do you use the Sign Language?" they nearly always say "No."

The first question of most persons is "What is it?" It is a simple method of asking questions and giving answers, that is talking, by means of the hands.

Not long ago I asked a boy whether the policemen on the crowded streets used Sign Language. He said, "No!" at least he did not know if they did.

I replied: "When the officer on Fifth Avenue wishes to *stop* all vehicles, what does he do?"

"He raises his hand, flat with palm forward," was the reply.

"Yes, and when he means 'come on,' what does he do?"

"He beckons this way."

"And how does he say 'go left, go right, go back, come, hurry up, you get out?'" Each of these signs I found was well known to the boy.

The girls are equally adept and equally unconscious of it.

One very shy little miss—so shy that she dared not speak—furnished a good illustration of this:

"Do you use the Sign Language in your school?" I asked.

She shook her head.

"Do you learn any language but English?"

She nodded.

"What is the use of learning any other than English?"

She raised her right shoulder in the faintest possible shrug.

"Now," was my reply, "don't you see you have already given me three signs of the Sign Language, which you said you did not use?"

Here are some of the better known. Each boy will probably find that he has known and used them all his schooldays:

You (pointing at the person);

Me (pointing at one's self);

Yes (nod);

No (head shake);

Go (move hand forward, palm first);

Come (draw hand toward one's self, palm in);

Hurry (same, but the hand quickly and energetically moved several times);

Come for a moment (hand held out back down, fingers closed except first, which is hooked and straightened quickly several times);

Stop (one hand raised, flat; palm forward);

Gently or *Go easy* (like "stop," but hand gently waved from side to side);

Good-bye (hand high, flat, palm down, fingers wagged all together);

Up (forefinger pointed and moved upward);

Down (ditto downward);

Silence or *hush* (forefinger across lips);

Listen (flat hand behind ear);

Whisper (silently move lips, holding flat hand at one side of mouth);

Friendship (hands clasped);

Threatening (fist shaken at person);

Warning (forefinger gently shaken at a slight angle toward person);

He is cross (forefinger crossed level);

Shame on you (right forefinger drawn across left toward person several times);

Scorn (turning away and throwing an imaginary handful of sand toward person);

Insolent defiance (thumb to nose tip, fingers fully spread);

Surrender (both hands raised high and flat to show no weapons);

Crazy (with forefinger make a little circle on forehead then point to person);

Look there (pointing);

Applause (silently make as though clapping hands);

Victory (one hand high above head as though waving hat);

Indifference (a shoulder shrug);

Ignorance (a shrug and headshake combined);

Pay (hand held out half open, forefinger and thumb rubbed together);

Poverty (both hands turned flat forward near trouser pockets);

Knife (first and second fingers of right hand used as to whittle first finger of left);

I am thinking it over (forefinger on right brow and eyes raised);

I forgot (touch forehead with all right finger tips, then draw flat hand past eyes once and shake head);

I send you a kiss (kiss finger tips and move hand in graceful sweep toward person);

The meal was good (pat stomach);

I beg of you (flat hands tight together and upright);

Upon my honor (with forefinger make a cross over heart);

Give me (hold out open flat hand pulling it back a little to finish);

I give you (the same, but push forward to finish);

Give me my bill (same, then make motion of writing);

Get up (raise flat hand sharply, palm upward);

Sit down (drop flat hand sharply, palm down);

Rub it out (quickly shake flat hand from side to side, palm forward);

Thank you (a slight bow, smile and hand-salute, made by drawing flat hand a few inches forward and downward palm up);

Will you? or, *is it so?* (eyebrows raised and slight bow made)

Query. The sign for *Question*—that is, "I am asking you a question," "I want to know"—is much used and important. Hold up the right hand toward the person, palm forward, fingers open, slightly curved and spread. Wave the hand gently by wrist action from side to side. It is used before, and sometimes after all questions. If you are very near, merely raise the eyebrows.

The following are needed in asking questions:

How Many? First the *Question* sign, then hold the left hand open, curved, palm up, fingers spread, then with right digit quickly tap each finger of left in succession, closing it back toward the left palm, beginning with the little finger.

How Much? Same as *How many?*

What? What are you doing? What do you want? What is it? First give *Question*, then hold right hand palm down, fingers slightly bent and separated, and, pointing forward, throw it about a foot from right to left several times, describing an arc upward.

When? If seeking a definite answer as to length of time, make signs for *Question*,

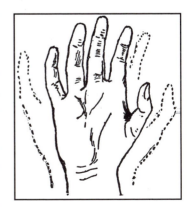

QUERY SIGN

How much, and then specify time by sign for hours, days, etc. When asking in general "*When*" for a date, hold the left index extended and vertical, other and thumb closed, make a circle around left index tip with tip of extended right index, others and thumb closed; and when the index reaches the starting point, stop it and point at tip of left index (what point of shadow?).

Where? (What direction) *First Question*, then with forefinger sweep the horizon in a succession of bounds, a slight pause at the bottom of each.

Which? First Question, then hold left hand in front of you with palm toward you, fingers to right and held apart; place the end of the right forefinger on that of left forefinger, and then draw it down across the other fingers.

Why? Make the sign for *Question*, then repeat it very slowly.

Who? First Question, and then describe with the right forefinger a small circle six inches in front of the mouth.

Eat. Throw the flat hand several times past the mouth in a curve.

Drink. Hold the right hand as though holding a cup near the mouth and tip it up.

Sleep. Lay the right cheek on the right flat hand.

My, mine, yours, possession, etc. Hold out the closed fist, thumb up, and swing it down a little so thumb points forward.

House. Hold the flat hands together like a roof.

Finished or *done.* Hold out the flat left hand palm to the right, then with flat right hand chop down past the ends of the left fingers.

Thus "*Will you eat?*" would be a *Question, you eat*, but *Have you eaten* would be, *Question, you eat, finished.*

Way or *road.* Hold both flat hands nearly side by side, palms up, but right one nearer the breast, then alternately lift them forward and draw them back to indicate track or feet traveling.

The Native American had much use for certain signs in describing the white trader. The first was:

Liar. Close the right hand except the first and second fingers; these are straight and spread; bring the knuckles of the first finger to the mouth, then pass it down forward to the left, meaning double or forked tongue.

The second sign, meaning "*very*" or "*very much,*" is made by striking the right fist down past the knuckles of the left without quite touching them, the left being held still.

Another useful sign is *time*. This is made by drawing a circle with the right forefinger on the back of the left wrist. It looks like a reference to the wrist watch, but it is certainly much older than that style of time-piece and probably refers to the shadow of a tree. Some prefer to draw the circle on the left palm as it is held up facing forward.

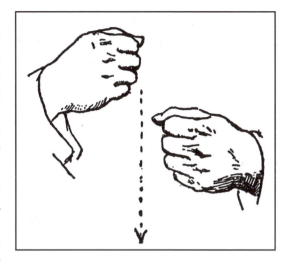

SIGN FOR VERY MUCH

If you wish to ask, "*What time is it?*" You make the signs *Question*, then *Time*. If the answer is "Three o'clock," you would signal:

Time and hold up *three* fingers of the right hand.

Hours are shown by laying the right forefinger as a pointer on the flat palm of the left and carrying it once around; *minutes* by moving the pointer a very little to the left.

If you wish to signal in answer 3:15. You give the signs for hours 3 and minutes 15. Holding all ten fingers up for 10, then those of one hand for 5.

It takes a good-sized dictionary to give all the signs in use, and a dictionary you must have, if you would become an expert.

First among the trail signs that are used by woodsmen and most likely to be of use are axe blazes on tree trunks. Among these some may vary greatly with locality, but there is one that I have found everywhere in use with scarcely any variation. That is the simple white spot meaning, "*Here is the trail.*"

The Native American in making it may nick off a speck of bark with his knife, the trapper with his hatchet may make it as big as a half-dollar, or the settler with his heavy axe may slab off half the tree-side; but the sign is the same in principle and in meaning, on trunk, log or branch from Atlantic to Pacific and from Hudson Strait to Rio Grande. "This is your trail," it clearly says in the universal language of the woods.

There are two ways of employing it: one when it appears on back and front of the trunk, so that the trail can be run both ways; the other when it appears on but one side of each tree, making a *blind trail*, which can be run one way only, the blind trail is often used by trappers and prospectors, who do not wish any one to follow their back track.

But there are treeless regions where the trail must be marked; regions of brush and sand, regions of rock, stretches of stone, and level wastes of grass. Here other methods must be employed.

A well-known Native American device, in the brush, is to break a twig and leave it hanging. (*Second line.*)

Among stones and rocks the recognized sign is one stone set on top of another (*top line*) and in places where there is nothing but grass the custom is to twist a tussock into a knot (*third line.*)

In running a trail one naturally looks straight ahead for the next sign; if the trail turned abruptly without notice one might easily be set wrong, but custom has provided against this. The tree blaze for turn "to the right" is shown in number 2, fourth row; "to the left" in number 3. The greater length of the turning blaze seems to be due to a desire for emphasis as the same mark set square on, is understood to mean "Look out, there is something of special importance here." Combined with a long side chip it means "very important; here turn aside." This is often used to mean "camp is close by," and a third sign that is variously combined but always with the general meaning of "warning" or "something of great importance" is a threefold blaze. (number 4 on fourth line.) The combination (number 1 on bottom row) would read "Look out now for something of great importance to the right." This blaze I have often seen used by trappers to mark the whereabouts of their trap or cache.

Surveyors often use a similar mark—that is, three simple spots and a stripe to mean, "There is a stake close at hand," while a similar blaze on another tree near by means that the stake is on a line between.

STONE SIGNS

These signs done into stone-talk refer to the top line of the chart.

These are often used in the Rockies where the trail goes over stony places or along stretches of slide-rock.

GRASS AND TWIG SIGNS

In grass the top of the tuft is made to show the direction to be followed; if it is a point of great importance three tufts are tied, their tops straight if the trail goes straight on; otherwise the tops are turned in the direction toward which the course turns.

Woodland tribes use twigs for a great many of these signs. (See second row.) The hanging broken twig, like the simple blaze, means "This is the trail." The twig clean broken off and laid on the ground across the line of march means, "Here break from your straight course and go in the line of the butt end," and when an especial *warning* is meant, the butt is pointed toward the one following the trail and raised somewhat, in a forked twig. If the butt of the twig were raised and pointing to the left, it would mean "Look out, camp, or ourselves, or the enemy, or the game we have killed is out that way." With some, the elevation of the butt is made to show the distance of the object; if low the object is near, if raised very high the object is a long way off.

These are the principal signs of the trail used by Scouts, Native Americans, and hunters in most parts of America. These are the standards—the ones sure to be seen by those who camp in the wilderness.

SMOKE SIGNALS

There is in addition a useful kind of sign that has been mentioned already in these papers—that is, the smoke signal. These were used chiefly by the Plains Indians.

A clear hot fire was made, then covered with green stuff or rotten wood so that it sent up a solid column of black smoke. By spreading and lifting a blanket over this smudge the column could be cut up into pieces long or short, and by a preconcerted code these could be made to convey tidings.

But the simplest of all smoke codes and the one of chief use to the Western traveler is this:

One steady smoke—"Here is camp."

Two steady smokes—"I am lost, come and help me."

I find two other smoke signals, namely:

Three smokes in a row—"Good news."

Four smokes in a row—"All are summoned to council."

These latter I find not of general use, nor are they so likely to be of service as the first two given.

SIGNAL BY SHOTS

The old buffalo hunters had an established signal that is still used by the mountain guides. It is as follows:

Two shots in rapid succession, an interval of five seconds by the watch, then one shot; this means, "where are you?" The answer given at once and exactly the same means "Here I am; what do you want?" The reply to this may be one shot, which means, "All right; I only wanted to know where you were." But if the reply repeats the first it means, "I am in serious trouble; come as fast as you can."

SPECIAL SIGNS

The Indians sometimes marked a spot of unusual importance by sinking the skull of a deer or a mountain sheep deep into a living tree, so that the horns hung out on each side. In time the wood and bark grew over the base of the horns and "medicine tree" was created. Several of these trees have become of historic importance.

UNIVERSAL SIGN ALPHABET

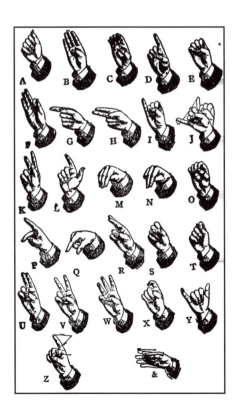

SEMAPHORE

MORSE CODE

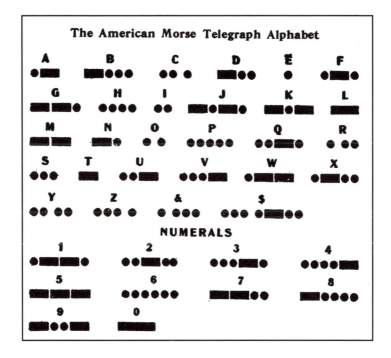

HIEROGLYPHS

ANCIENT EGYPT.	
The following alphabet will furnish a general idea of the hiero-glyphical homophones, as well as of the phonetic value of each sym	bol. I append to this table a Coptic alph

COPTIC ALPHABET.

Ⲁ	ⲁ	Alpha	A
Ⲃ	ⲃ	Vida	B
Ⲅ	ⲅ	Gamma	Gʜ
Ⲇ	ⲇ	Dalda	D
Ⲉ	ⲉ	Ei	E
Ⲍ	ⲍ	Zida	Z
Ⲏ	ⲏ	Hida	Eʜ
Ⲑ	ⲑ	Thida	Tʜ
Ⲓ	ⲓ	Iauda	I
Ⲕ	ⲕ	Kabba	K
Ⲗ	ⲗ	Laula	L
Ⲙ	ⲙ	Mi	M
Ⲛ	ⲛ	Ni	N
Ⲝ	ⲝ	Exi	X
Ⲟ	ⲟ	O	O
Ⲡ	ⲡ	Pi	P
Ⲣ	ⲣ	Ro	R
Ⲥ	ⲥ	Sima	S
Ⲧ	ⲧ	Dau	D.T.
Ⲩ	ⲩ	Ue	U.V
Ⲫ	ⲫ	Phi	Pʜ
Ⲭ	ⲭ	Chi	Hʜ
Ⲯ	ⲯ	Epei	Ps
Ⲱ	ⲱ	O	O
Ⲟⲩ	ⲩ	Shei	Sʜ
Ϥ	ϥ	Fei	F
Ϧ	ϧ	Khei	Kʜ
Ϩ	ϩ	Hori	H
Ϫ	ϫ	Sjansja	Sⱼ
Ϭ	ϭ	Ssima	Sₛ
Ϯ	ϯ	Dei	T

HIEROGLYPHIC ALPHA[

A, E, I, O, U,

B

K

T, Tʜ, D

L, R

M

N

F, Pʜ, P,

S

Sⱼ, Sₛ

PH, V, Uo

Kʜ, Sʜ, X

Sʜ

Hʜ, H

Of the hieratic and demotic I have made no study, but the suc-ceeding inscriptions will indicate their appearance. It is the first line of a poem in the hieratic character from a papyrus now in the British Museum, commemorating the cam Sesostris—and his victories over several A from Egypt. Its date may be about 1550

SIMPLE MAGIC

SLEIGHT OF HAND

It is our intention to lay more stress upon those tricks which require no apparatus, than upon those for which special apparatus or the assistance of another is required. No one is so well pleased by a trick whose essence evidently lies in the machinery, while every one feels pleasure at seeing a sleight of hand trick.

THE TRAVELLED BALLS

This is always a favorite feat. You take three or four cups, you place them upon a table, and exhibit an equal number of balls.

You put a cup over each ball, and cover them from sight. You then take each ball separately and fling it in the air. After the third ball has been thus flung away, you take up the cups again, and, to the surprise of the spectators, the three balls have come back again, and each is found under and presently find it under another cup; and, lastly, you bring all the three under the same cup.

The secret of this capital trick lies chiefly in the *fourth* ball, the existence of which the audience do not know.

Before you begin, put a fourth ball in some place where you can easily get at it,—in your pocket, for example, or stuck on a little spike fastened to your own side of the table: throw the three balls on the table, and while you are handling the cups with the left hand, and shifting the

balls about in them, quietly get the truth ball into the right hand, and hold it at the roots of the second and third fingers. You will now find that with the tips of those fingers you can pick the ball out of the palm of the hand. Being thus prepared you may begin the trick.

Put a ball under each cup, and be careful to get the balls close to the edge of the cup which is farthest from you. Let them stay there while you talk to your audience in some flourishing style, and, in the mean time, get the fourth ball between the *tips* of your second and third fingers; keep these fingers well doubled into the palm, take the right-hand cup between thumb and forefinger, keeping the rest of the fingers behind it, lift it off ball, and as you set it down, neatly slip the fourth ball under it. As you will now have your hands quite empty, it may be as well to make some gesture which shows that you have nothing concealed.

Take up the first ball, and say that it is going to Europe. Draw your hand quickly back, as if to throw, and while doing so drop the ball into the palm of the hand and catch it between the roots of the fingers, just as the forth ball was held. Pretend to throw it away, opening your hand as if you did so, but taking care to hold it tightly in the finger-roots. Take up the second cup slip the first ball under it as before, and proceed to do so with the third, pretending each time to throw the ball away. Take up the last of the three balls which have now come back again.

Replace the cups over the balls and as you do so slip the ball in your hand under the left-hand cup, so that there will be two balls in it. Take up the right-hand cup, pretend to throw the ball into the middle cup, pick it up and show the two balls there. As you replace the cup, slip the concealed ball into it, so as to bring three under one cup, and proceed as before. When you have finished the performance, by showing the three balls under one cup, get rid of the fourth ball by sticking it on the projecting needle.

PALMING A COIN

This phrase involves an explanation of the first grand principles of the art, without which no feat of mere sleight of hand with coin can be successfully performed. The exhibitor, before commencing, should turn back the sleeves of his coat, to avoid the appearance of passing any thing down the arm, and may then prepare himself for the first illusion in the manner following:—

Place a coin, either a dime or a quarter, on the *tips* of the middle and third fingers, so that it may rest there of its own weight. By now turning the hand with the knuckles uppermost, and quickly closing the fingers into the palm, the coin may be held securely by the contraction of the thumb, and the hand still appear to contain nothing. This is *palming*, and with a little practice nearly every feat of simple legerdemain may be performed by its means. Care, of course, must be taken not to expose the coin by any reversed movement of the hand.

Securing the coin in the right hand, and simultaneously making it appear to pass into the left, the exhibitor may cause it either to disappear altogether, or, by holding a glass in the right hand, bid it fly from the left into the tumbler, where the expansion of the thumb will readily cause it to fall. This feat, when skilfully performed, never fails to elicit surprise and admiration.

TO BRING TWO SEPARATE COINS INTO ONE HAND

Take two cents, which must be carefully placed in each hand, as thus: The right hand with the coin on the tips of the Index and middle finger, and the left hand with the coin in the palm. Then place, at a short distance from each other, both hands open on the table, the left palm being level with the fingers of the right. By now suddenly turning the hands over, the cent from the right hand will fly, without being perceived, into the palm of the left, and make the transit appear most unaccountable to the bewildered eyes of the spectators. By placing the audience in front, and not at the side of the exhibitor, this illusion, if neatly performed, can never be detected.

THE MAGIC HANDKERCHIEF

Take any handkerchief and put a quarter or a dime into it. Fold it up, laying the four corners over it so that it is entirely hidden by the last one. Ask the audience to *touch and feel the coin* inside. Then unfold it, and the coin has disappeared without anybody seeing it removed. The method is as follows:

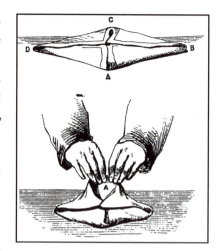

Take a dime, and privately stick a piece of wax on one side of it; place it in the center of the handkerchief, with *the waxed side up;* at the same time bring the corner of the handkerchief marked A, and completely hide the coin; this should be carefully done, or the audience will discover the wax. Squeeze the coin very hard, so that by means of the wax it sticks to the handkerchief; then fold the corners, B, C, and D, leaving A open.

Having done this, take hold of the handkerchief with both hands, as represented in Figure at the opening, A, and sliding along your fingers at the edge of the same, the handkerchief becomes unfolded, the coin adheres to it, coming into your right hand. Detach it, shake the handkerchief out, and the coin will have disappeared. To convince the audience the coin is in the handkerchief, drop it on the table, and it will sound against the wood. This is an easy trick.

HOW TO TALK TO GIRLS

So, how do you talk to girls? It's a good question, though not necessarily an easy one. I've lived for a bit over a half century now but I can't swear I know the answer. Even at my great age, I still find myself occasionally flummoxed in the presence of a female. I bet the same is true of you.

Say you want to talk to a girl, unfortunately it often goes something like this, doesn't it?

Your palms are wet, your mouth is dry. You stand there tongue-tied. You stare at your shoes, you shuffle your feet, and for your very life, you can not think of a thing to say. Or worse—out of pure nervousness—you say the first dumb thing that comes into your head. Then, recognizing your mistake, you try to make up for it by blurting out something that to your anguished ears sounds even dumber. Stop, you cry to yourself, 'Stop!' But you cannot stop, and in a moment you are babbling like a brook. Usually what you wind up saying is inappropriate, or rude—sometimes it is even downright disgusting. But you just can't seem to help yourself. There's just something about some girls.

Nowadays people generally take Mark Twain's Tom Sawyer as a model American boy. It might be instructive to check-out how he manages this tricky task.

There's a new girl in town, named Becky Thatcher, and Tom would like to get to know her. His first move is to get her to notice him.

He worshipped this new angel with furtive eye, till he saw that she had discovered him; then he pretended he did not know she was present, and began to "show off" in all sorts of absurd boyish ways, in order to win her admiration. He kept up this grotesque foolishness for some time; but by-and-by, while he was in the midst of some dangerous gymnastic performances, he glanced aside and saw that the little girl was wending her way toward the house. Tom came up to the fence and leaned on it, grieving, and hoping she would tarry yet awhile longer. She halted a moment on the steps and then moved toward the door. Tom heaved a great sigh as she put her foot on the threshold. But his face lit up, right away, for she tossed a pansy over the fence a moment before she disappeared.

He returned, now, and hung about the fence till nightfall, "showing off," as before; but the girl never exhibited herself again, though Tom comforted himself a little with the hope that she had been near some window, meantime, and been aware of his attentions. Finally he strode home reluctantly, with his poor head full of visions.

Next day in school, Tom gets his chance with Becky.

Presently the boy began to steal furtive glances at the girl. She observed it, "made a mouth" at him and gave him the back of her head for the space of a minute. When she cautiously faced around again, a peach lay before her. She thrust it away. Tom gently put it back. She thrust it away again, but with less animosity. Tom patiently returned it to its place. Then she let it remain. Tom scrawled on his slate, "Please take it—I got more." The girl glanced at the words, but made no sign. Now the boy began to draw something on the slate, hiding his work with his left hand. For a time the girl refused to notice; but her human curiosity presently began to manifest itself by hardly perceptible signs.

The boy worked on, apparently unconscious. The girl made a sort of noncommittal attempt to see, but the boy did not betray that he was aware of it. At last she gave in and hesitatingly whispered:

"Let me see it."

Tom partly uncovered a dismal caricature of a house with two gable ends to it and a corkscrew of smoke issuing from the chimney. Then the girl's interest began to fasten itself upon the work and she forgot everything else. When it was finished, she gazed a moment, then whispered:

"It's nice—make a man."

The artist erected a man in the front yard, that resembled a derrick. He could have stepped over the house; but the girl was not hypercritical; she was satisfied with the monster, and whispered:

"It's a beautiful man—now make me coming along."

Tom drew an hour-glass with a full moon and straw limbs to it and armed the spreading fingers with a portentous fan. The girl said:

"It's ever so nice—I wish I could draw."

"It's easy," whispered Tom, "I'll learn you."

"Oh, will you? When?"

"At noon. Do you go home to dinner?"

"I'll stay if you will."

"Good—that's a whack. What's your name?"

"Becky Thatcher. What's yours? Oh, I know. It's Thomas Sawyer."

"That's the name they lick me by. I'm Tom when I'm good. You call me Tom, will you?"

"Yes."

Now Tom began to scrawl something on the slate, hiding the words from the girl. But she was not backward this time. She begged to see. Tom said:

"Oh, it ain't anything."

"Yes it is."

"No it ain't. You don't want to see."

"Yes I do, indeed I do. Please let me."

"You'll tell."

"No I won't—deed and deed and double deed won't."

"You won't tell anybody at all? Ever, as long as you live?"

"No, I won't ever tell anybody. Now let me."

"Oh, you don't want to see!"

"Now that you treat me so, I will see." And she put her small hand upon his and a little scuffle ensued, Tom pretending to resist in earnest but letting his hand slip by degrees till these words were revealed: "I love You."

"Oh, you bad thing!" And she hit his hand a smart rap, but reddened and looked pleased, nevertheless.

Tom is smooth, and he doesn't let the fact that he likes this Becky get in his way, instead she is his inspiration to be bold and honest and attentive and playful. He relates to her as he would to any person he likes. He doesn't see her as a girl, but as an individual, and that's why they click.

Incidentally, by chapter's end, Becky and Tom are engaged to one another and have even sealed the deal with a kiss. Fast work for a ten-year-old. Now, a kiss may not be exactly what you have in mind—doesn't matter, we can still take the lesson from Tom. The best answer is also the simplest. It's easiest to talk to a girl when you recognize her as an individual person, and don't worry because she happens to be a girl also.

ON COWBOYING

By Fay E. Ward

EVOLUTION OF THE COWBOY

The evolution of the American cowboy and his equipment dates back to the Spanish conquest of Mexico in 1519 by Cortés and his conquistadors. The descendants of these same adventurous conquistadors settled in Mexico. Some of them became owners of large estates and were known as *hacendados*, and their extensive ranches were called *haciendas*. Eventually they drifted northward with their great herds of longhorn cattle and mustang horses and crossed the Rio Bravo, now called the Rio Grande.

The stock industry thrived and spread from Texas to California, and there naturally came into being a great number of stockmen who operated on a smaller scale than the *hacendados*. They were known as rancheros, or small ranch owners. The men who were employed to handle the range stock were known as *vaqueros*, meaning cowboys. The term "buckaroo" in common use in the West is derived from this Spanish word.

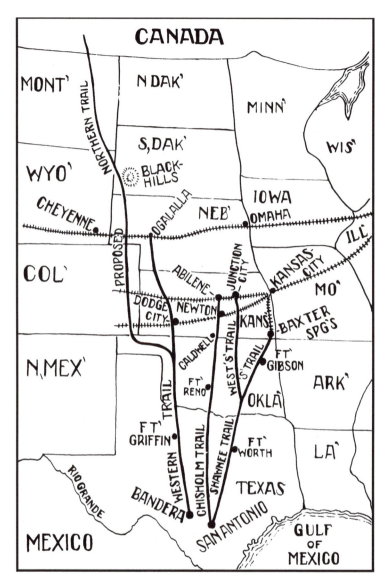

THE OLD CATTLE TRAILS

When Texas gained her independence in 1836, the American cowboy came into being. The Mexican ranchers abandoned their ranches and drifted *muy pronto* across the Rio Grande to avoid the wrath of the *Tejanos*. Even before the departure of the Mexican ranchers, and as early as the first Spanish settlements in Texas, a great many horses and a large number of cattle escaped and went wild in the brush. Since the

Spaniards did not castrate their animals, these escaped horses and cattle multiplied rapidly, so that, together with the animals the Mexicans abandoned when they trekked back across the border, the wild herds became incredibly numerous. The great number of horses and cattle running wild tempted many a buffalo hunter and Indian scout to go into the cattle business, for cattle and horses were to be had for the taking.

Naturally the Americans adopted the equipment and methods used by the Mexican rancheros and *vaqueros*. Therefore, the style of equipment used by the early-day buffalo hunters and scouts had its influence, to a certain extent, upon the outfits used by the old-time cowhand that followed. The illustrations show the various stages of development of the cowhand's equipment.

During the Civil War many of the ranchers and cowhands deserted the ranches and enlisted in the service of the Confederate army. As a consequence, the cattle and horses that were left to range unmolested increased to even greater numbers and ran wild over a vast territory. When the war was over, many of the former cowmen returned to their old occupation and with them came ex-soldiers, their friends and friends of their friends who saw that here was a great opportunity to build up independent stock businesses. When the northern trails were opened, the Texas cowhand came into his own. It is estimated that fully ninety percent of the old-time Texas cowhands were former Confederate soldiers.

During the period from 1865 to 1895, the cowhand and his equipment changed materially. In California the Spanish methods and equipment retained their influence upon the outfits of the cowhand much longer than in any other part of the cow country north of the Mexican Border.

When the northern trails were closed, the northern cowhand became an important factor in the cattle businesses, and the equipment and methods he used were the result of Texas and California influences. But these influences, when fused with and then modified by conditions of climate and locale, produced a distinct type, as easily distinguishable and recognizable as its Texas or California counterparts.

However, Texas, California and Montana cowhands are the same kind of guys under the skin; they differ, actually, only in the style of their equipment and in the methods used in their work, which are

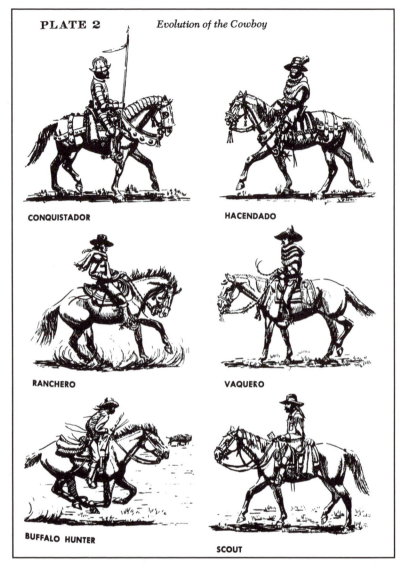

PLATE 2   *Evolution of the Cowboy*

CONQUISTADOR

HACENDADO

RANCHERO

VAQUERO

BUFFALO HUNTER

SCOUT

largely shaped by the kind of country they operate in and the sort of weather they have to face.

The species "cowhand" is no special breed of human; but he is a special type created by his special way of life. Perhaps, though, it does take a special kind of guy to choose to be a cowhand. The cowhand is possessed by a sort of pioneering spirit; he likes nature—that is, nature in the raw. He doesn't mind taking a chance, win or lose. He can take it on the chin and keep coming back for more.

TEXAS COWHAND OF 1870

EARLY CALIFORNIA-NEVADA HAND

MONTANA OR NORTHERN COWHAND

SOUTHWESTERN TYPE OF RIDER

MODERN RODEO ROPER

MODERN RODEO BRONC RIDER

The cowhand and the stock range are as closely identified with each other as the cowhand and his horse. Anything written about the evolution of the cowboy assumes that the reader has some knowledge of the history of the cow country and the stock business. The author realizes that the short outline presented above does not cover the subject adequately. However, he hopes it will help in the understanding of the pages that follow which have, moreover, been made as self-explanatory as possible.

The professional rodeo* hand is also a product of the cow country, generally speaking, and is of the same type as the average cowhand. As a rule he is a "top-hand" and was schooled in the actual work of riding and roping out where skyscrapers seldom grow. Because of the inducements offered in cash prizes to the winners of the various roping and riding events and the thrill of winning over the best men in the game, some of the finest riders and ropers have become professional rodeo contestants and have made history which will long be remembered. The rodeo or frontier-contest hand has become a popular figure wherever he is seen in action.

Rodeo work is highly specialized and every move that a contestant makes is carefully planned to save time. The equipment used is designed and arranged to promote speed and efficiency. The element of chance, which may stand between the rodeo artist and the winning of the contest, is far greater than in any other line of sport. And there are always many keen competitors for the prizes. Rodeo work is more dangerous, too, than any other sport at present featured before the American public.

TYPES OF RANGE STOCK

The different breeds of horses and cattle which have been predominant in the cow country since the beginning of the stock industry are shown to some extent in the illustrations on Plate 4.

The mustang and the longhorn are of Spanish origin; they are the descendants of the cattle and horses which Cortés and the other conquistadors brought over from Spain in 1519 (the date of the conquest of Mexico) and during the years that followed. The Spanish horse was of Moorish and Arabian origin. The original Arab strain had great endurance and certainly many of the Indian horses in the early 1800's showed this quality. The cattle were for the most part of the Andalusian breed.

The mustang evolved from a process of inbreeding that went on among the horses that escaped from the Spaniards and lapsed into a wild state. Very few of them ever made good cow horses because they lacked the great stamina and endurance needed for cow work. Generally speaking, they were narrow-chested, light-boned and droop-rumped.

---

* Pronounced rodeo by the cowhand, cattleman and others identified with the cattle business; and rodéo by some outsiders who have adopted the Spanish pronunciation.

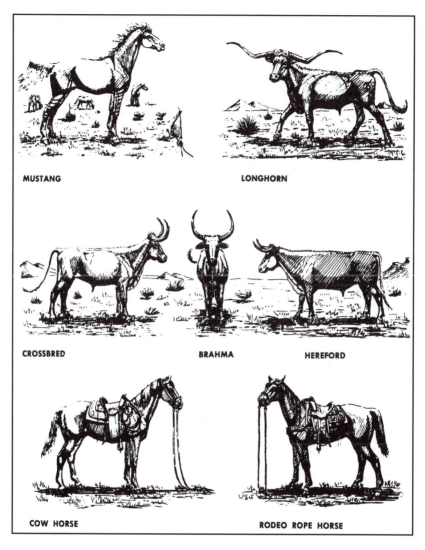

PLATE:4 THE EVOLUTION OF BREEDS

This deterioration of the mustang can be ascribed to the fact that many of the best stallions were killed or badly injured in the fights between them during the mating season. What brought the wild mustangs of the Navajo country down in size more than anything else was probably the fact that they suffered from undernourishment. Also, the screwworm's ravages contributed to the decimation of the best sires. So, for the most part, only the weaker specimens were left to propagate the species.

The Mexican horse, which is often referred to as the Spanish pony, and the Indian pony are descendants of the mustang; they are distinct breeds even though they have this common ancestry. Generally the Mexican or Spanish pony shows certain marked characteristics such as black stripes running down the length of the back and across the shoulders; frequently there are also black or dark-colored stripes or bars on the forelegs. The prevailing colorings are *grulla* (gru-ya), smoky blue or mouse color; *palomina*, a golden cream color; *appalusa*, a sort of bluish or red-roan color with spots of pure color juxtaposed in striking contrasts. Browns or buckskins are common colors, too. These Mexican or Spanish ponies are capable of great endurance and make good saddle horses.

The Indian pony is a decided improvement over the Mexican horse, both as to conformation and disposition. He is a blocky, well-proportioned horse, and because of the Indians' partiality for the pinto (paint), this type of horse has, through selection, been widely propagated among Indian ponies. The colors of the "paint" are generally white and black or white and bay, each color in its purity, so that there is a strong contrast between them.

The modern range horse and cow horse is the result of crossbreeding the Mexican or Spanish pony mares with the saddle horse—Thoroughbred, standard-bred and purebred sires. In the northern sections of the cow country the breeding trend is toward a large-boned, blocky and clean-limbed type of horse. The Percheron sire is the type of horse used. In the southwest, the qualities mostly favored in a good cow horse are conformation, endurance and speed. The Thoroughbred and the quarter-horse types of sire are much in evidence.

The rodeo roping horse and the horses generally used for bulldogging purposes are of the quarter-horse type. They are very compact, clean-limbed and powerful. For short distances of up to one quarter of a mile, this type of horse has no equal for speed. This is a desirable quality for a roping horse.

The longhorn breed of cattle is also the outcome of inbreeding among the animals in their wild state. These cattle that escaped from the Spaniards were of Andalusian strain, the same breed that provides the famous bulls of the Spanish bull ring. Longhorns are of many colors, including *appalusas*, *grullas*, browns and duns, as well as blues and red-roans and blacks. They are among the sturdiest of all the cattle breeds;

they can go farther to water and grass, and still thrive, more than any other type of cattle to be found on the North American continent. The longhorn dominated the range until the late 19th century. By crossing the Durham and the Hereford with the longhorn, a crossbred type of range cattle was produced which proved to be a good "rustler" and a good beef producer. The crossbred cattle are high-horned and easier to handle than the longhorns.

The Texas Brahma is also a crossbred type of range critter. It has been experimented with in the coastal regions of south Texas and in some parts of the southwest. It is the result of a cross between the longhorn, the Brahma cattle of India, and the Hereford. Texas Brahmas are very thrifty and are immune to ticks. They are wild-natured and difficult to handle in rough country and, because of their color, they have been widely discriminated against by cattle buyers. The colors are mixtures of brown and light cream which have been hard to erase in crossbreeding, but a fixed, blood-red color has been obtained by a few breeders. They are high-withered, because of the hump on the Brahma, and they are also droop-rumped and droop-eared. Because of their wild disposition and their ability to jump high and crooked, they are used extensively in rodeos and frontier contests for riding purposes. Their horns curve vertically above their heads, which helps to give them a wild and scary expression.

The Hereford, or white-face, has become the standard breed of range cattle because of qualities which make for a better type of beef carcass and because of their general adaptability to range conditions in the different sections of the cow country. They are light-boned and lower in stature than the other types of cattle mentioned herein, and though they are not as thrifty as the other types, their color and uniformity are more important qualities.

RANCH WORK

A brief summary of the different kinds of work that a cowboy is called upon to do in different seasons of the year, in the north and in the south, is outlined in the following paragraphs.

Northern ranch work: In the spring, riding bog is the job of keeping weak stock pulled out of the mud or bog holes. Stock which has become weak by springtime, especially the old cows, is easily bogged down. While crowding around some small water hole, weak stock is often knocked down by the stronger animals and is not able to get up. It is then necessary to pull them out at the end of a catch rope. The best way to pull a bogged critter out of a hole is to pitch a loop over its horns—not around its neck—and then pull it straight out on its back. This is better than to try to pull the animal out sideways or straight ahead with its legs under it. It is often necessary, if the animal has been bogged down for some time, for the rider to wade in and pull the critter's legs out of the mud before a horse can haul it out. Once the critter is out, it is generally necessary for the rider to tail the animal up (pull it up by the tail) to get it on its feet. Generally, once it is standing, it will try to turn and charge its rescuer. By watching his chance, the rider can get away from the critter by going off directly behind it. Sometimes it is necessary for two riders to lift an animal to its feet; one gets ahold of its horns and the other gets a tail hold. The man in front makes his getaway while the man behind holds the critter back. When the front man is safe, the other man high-tails it for *his* horse which is off at a safe distance where the steer can't easily charge him right away, and so both hands escape the irate animal.

Gathering weak stock is another job which the cowhand is often required to do in early spring when feed is scarce and it is necessary to feed the animals. Cows with early calves often need feeding to keep them going and those that have been weakened from being bogged down have to be gathered and fed. Weak stock has to be handled easy. Give them plenty of time and don't crowd them and then they will travel better.

Cleaning out water holes is sometimes necessary, though not often. A team and slip (scraper) are generally used to do the work which may take as much as a week, or only a day, depending on the country and the water supply.

Riding fence is sometimes part of the job of working for a barbwire outfit. Here is where a pair of wire-plyers takes the place of a six-shooter.

Breaking horses is generally done by a professional bronc snapper, but often a cowhand breaks out three or four head that look good to him for his own personal use; these horses he is then allowed to ride as part of his string. Young horses are generally easily broken. If plenty of time is taken in handling them and they are given good treatment, they will seldom make a jump.

Calf work is spring wagon work (roundup), and consists of gathering and branding calves. The interval between the spring and fall roundup work is often filled by two or three weeks of haying or fence riding and a number of other jobs that have nothing to do with handlin' a rope or a gun. Some cowhands have been known to take a short vacation during this season until the fall work is ready to start.

Fall work generally starts with beef work, that is, the job of rounding up and gathering beef cattle and other stock for shipment to market. At the same time, calves that were dropped after the spring calf work and any that may have been overlooked are branded and marked. Big outfits may make from two to four shipments during the season and keep a wagon busy gathering stock until snow falls.

Bulls are often gathered after beef work is ended so they can be fed during the winter. Calves are gathered and weaned in order to give their mothers a better chance to pull through the winter.

Winter work does not require as many hands as are needed in other seasons. The old hands—men who have made good—are the ones who are generally given a winter job. Gathering poor cows, cutting ice to open up water holes, feeding bulls and poor stock, hauling firewood, and riding line to keep stock from drifting off their range are the things which keep a stockhand from getting lonesome through the winter.

Line-camp work is practically the same as that done at the headquarters or home ranch. A line camp is located on the outer edge of an outfit's range and a couple of riders are posted there to look after poor stock and feed them, and to keep the water holes open by cutting the ice. They also ride line on the stock to keep it from drifting off its range. During storms cattle drift with the storm, and by cutting sign after a storm the line riders can generally tell whether any of the stock has drifted beyond the boundary of its range. If so, the riders locate them, ride them back and turn them loose where they belong.

A cowhand's mount in the winter consists of two horses which he calls his winter horses and which are kept up and fed grain. They are generally horses that a hand can pack a calf on if necessary and drive an old, poor cow with at the same time.

Southern ranch work: In presenting a brief outline of the work which a cowhand is expected to do in the southwestern range country, it must be remembered that ranching conditions vary greatly and that the methods of handling range stock and the kind of ranch work required depend on the type of country being worked and on the conditions of climate. Much of present-day ranch work is in fenced range territory; ranch work is different under these conditions from that in open range country. However, there is far more open range than the average individual realizes. It should be remembered that the general outline given in this section of the work that is done by cowhands covers the range country as a whole, closed or open.

Spring work is the gathering and feeding of weak stock, generally cows, either with their calves or heavy with calf. The condition of the stock depends on whether there has been an early or late spring, as well as on the range conditions during the winter. If the cattle winter well, very few will require feeding, but if they need it, they are given cotton-seed cake, sotol, burned prickly pear (cactus leaves with the spines burned off) and sometimes hay. Where local range conditions are poor, stock is often moved to another range until the grazing improves and the cattle can be brought back.

Riding fence is necessary where the range is enclosed. The job of keeping up a fence around a hundred-section★ ranch will keep a stock-hand from loafin' when other work is scarce.

Range riding is generally for picking up any calves that have not been branded and marked and to keep cases on the activities of any *hombres* who happen to be handy with a long rope and an outlaw hot iron. Then there is crippled or injured stock that screwworms have started to work on. These animals it is necessary to rope and bed down so that someone can doctor them. Screwworms are a constant source of trouble for the cowmen in the southwest during the warm months, from the first of June until the end of September. Blowflies will blow (lay their eggs in) a freshly exposed injury and a horde of screwworms will attack the area the same day the wound is blown. And if the animal attacked is not caught and doped (doctored) within a day or so, the worms will do great damage. Calves freshly branded and marked have to be closely watched and looked after until the wounds have healed because of the danger

---

★ A section is a square mile.

of screwworms getting into the exposed places, especially in the bag of a calf that has been cut (castrated). Riders pack a screwworm remedy in a little bottle attached to the saddle so it will always be handy when wanted. When the range rider finds a case of worms that needs doctoring, he ropes the animal, ties it down, and proceeds to shoot the dope into the affected part. The medicine used for this purpose exterminates the worms. It is generally a fly repellant and a healing antiseptic all in one. If there is no special worm medicine at hand when a case of worms has been found, the next best thing to do is to fill the wound with dry, pulverized cow chips or something similar that is locally available. This sort of substitute has proved effective at times when the wound is deep enough to hold the powdered material. Whatever is used should be tamped in closely in order to shut off the air from the worms. If the air can be cut off the worms will suffocate. This may not seem practical to some who have never tried such an emergency remedy, but it can work. (In the northern section of the range country the blowfly is not so prevalent as in the southern states, and consequently the danger from screwworms is minor compared to what it is in warmer climates.)

Water is always a problem that demands attention in the southwest and is often looked after by a rider while doing general ranch work. Where there are no running streams or natural water holes, windmills or dirt-tank reservoirs are depended upon to supply the water for the stock. If the water supply fails on some part of the outfit's range, it will become necessary to move the stock to some other locality. Windmills must be kept in operation, the outlet of the water supply source must be carefully watched to prevent loss of water, and so forth.

Roundup work, gathering yearlings for shipment, and branding and marking calves is a part of the spring work.

Summer work generally keeps a hand busy shootin' the dope to screwworms. Motherless calves are picked up and packed or driven to camp where they can be looked after. Bulls are scattered to different parts of the range wherever they are needed.

Fall work is practically the same as summer work; the same job of doctoring stock is continued until late in the season. During range branding, a rider must keep his eye peeled for sleepers (calves that have been earmarked by a rustler, but not branded; the rustler intends to return later to brand the calves with his own brand); it is necessary to look over every calf that is earmarked to make sure that it is packing a brand. Salt grounds must be watched and salt put out when the supply gets low. Breaking horses is a job often done in the fall when there is plenty of grass to keep them in shape while they are being handled.

Fall roundup work includes gathering calves for shipment to feeders who fatten them for baby beef. Old cows and dry or barren she-stuff are also gathered and shipped for slaughter.

Water problems, range riding, and fence riding occupy the stock-hand's time during the winter months. Roundup work and the gathering of calves for shipment is done in the winter by those outfits that did not ship calves in the fall. Also, bulls are gathered and placed in a separate pasture. Many of the big outfits have the hands break in horses during the winter. The horses are kept up and fed and this helps to gentle them so that when spring comes they are in good shape.

Telling the age of cattle by the horns and teeth: There are two ways by which the experienced cowhand can determine the age of range cattle, to wit, by reading the teeth and the horns. The diagrams on Plate 5 illustrate how the ages of cattle can be determined by both horns and teeth, though it is seldom necessary for a cowman to tooth a critter to determine its age, as most all range cattle have horns and the horn rings which are easily noted reveal the critter's years of growth.

The diagrams on the left of Plate 5 illustrate the growth and wear of the front teeth of the lower jaw of cattle. (Cattle have teeth only on the lower jaw.) The first set of teeth shown at the top of the Plate are those of a month-old calf. At birth the calf has two or more temporary or first sets of incisor teeth. With the first month the entire set of eight incisors has appeared as shown.

The diagram entitled "18 to 20 Months" shows how the temporary teeth have worn down; they will soon be replaced by permanent teeth.

The drawing entitled "2 Years" shows the third set of teeth with two permanent center pinchers which have replaced the two temporary incisors.

Now note the diagram entitled "3 Years." At two and a half to three years the permanent first intermediates are cut and are usually fully developed at the end of three years.

In the diagram "4 Years," the internal faces of the incisors as they look at four years are shown. At three and a half years the second teeth will have been cut and will be on a level with the first intermediates which will begin to wear at four years.

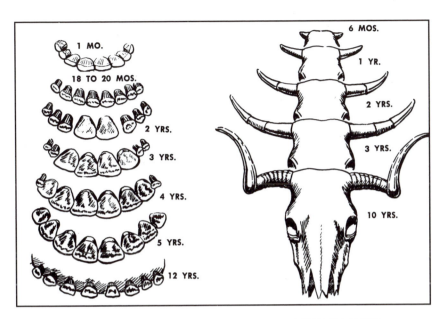

PLATE 5: TELLING THE AGE OF CATTLE BY THE HORNS AND TEETH

"5 Years": This diagram shows the teeth as they appear when the critter has reached maturity and is full mouthed. At four and a half to five years the corner teeth are replaced and the animal has a full complement of incisors with the corners fully developed.

At five to six years there is a leveling of the permanent pinchers and the corner incisors show wear. At seven to eight years the pinchers are noticeably worn, and at eight to nine years the middle pairs are worn. By ten years the corner teeth are worn.

After six years the arch or curve of the teeth gradually loses its rounded contour, and it becomes nearly straight by the twelfth year, as can be seen in the diagrams. In the meantime the teeth have become triangular in shape and distinctly separated, showing a progressive wearing down to stubs.

It is not difficult to tell the age of range cattle by their horns, as can be seen from the diagrams on the right of Plate 5. These diagrams show the development of the horns of a cow from the time she is eight months old until her tenth year. The way a critter's horns develop can be summed up as follows:

Two small, hard, rounded buttons, or points, emerge from the skin when the calf is eight to ten days old. At three weeks a little flexible horn has appeared. At five or six months the horn begins to curve and to assume a little of the shape it will eventually have. Up to this time, and during the first year, the horn is covered with an epidermic prolongation of the skin similar to that seen on a foal's hoof at birth. This covering dries and scales off by the twelfth or fifteenth month. Then the horn grows its permanent, natural, shining, tough surface and has the shape indicated in the diagram at "1 Year."

In the second year the horns start a second growth and a small groove is seen encircling the horn between the substance secreted the in first year and that developed in the second. A second ring appears during the third year. These two rings, or grooves, around the horn are not well marked and all traces of them disappear as the animal becomes older. From three years on, the growth of the horns is marked by a groove or ring that is much deeper and shows clearly as an elevation of horny substance around the horn. These rings provide an accurate basis for estimating the age of the animal. After the animal is three years old, the outer part of the horn plus the first ring or groove are counted as representing three years, and each subsequent ring toward the base of the horn is counted as representing one year. At the part of the diagram marked "10 Years," the horn is shown as having seven rings, with an eighth ring about to appear. The first ring represents three years, the six other rings indicate nine years in all, and the growth from the last ring shows that the animal is really ten years old. The rings are more distinct on the concave or front part of the horns. After an animal has reached nine years the horns have a tendency to become smaller at the base. To make *certain* of an animal's age, the teeth should also be taken into consideration.

Fighting prairie fires: In the states where the range is heavily sodded and covered with buffalo and other grasses, prairie fires are a menace to the cowmen who have constantly to keep a good eye peeled for any indication of smoke appearing on the horizon. In hot, dry seasons, when the grass is withered and dry, the danger of fire is perhaps greater than at any other time. A big fire sweeping across an outfit's range may cause untold damage and loss of stock.

The causes of fire are many; a fire may be started by a piece of glass, a dropped match, lightning, and so forth. At night a fire can be spotted a long way off by the reflection of light in the sky. By the direction the wind is blowing, one can tell which way the fire is traveling. If the fire is headed for an outfit's range, then all hands get busy and proceed to gather old slickers, sacks, pieces of saddle blankets, etc., to fight the fire with. Sometimes a wagon with several barrels of water is taken along if the country to be crossed is not too rough. The sacks and blankets are soaked in the water, but often water is not available and the fire is whipped out with dry sacks and blankets.

Where the fire is running in heavy grass and is fanned by a strong wind, more effective measures are necessary to battle and check it. A very effective technique often employed by cowmen is the following: A cow or horse is killed, the head is cut off and the carcass is split in half lengthwise. The two halves make two fire drags. Each half-carcass is turned so the inside will be down and ropes are attached to the forelegs and hind legs. These ropes are grasped by riders, two to each carcass section, and they drag the carcass over the flames on each side of the fire. Meanwhile the other men extinguish the sparks and small flames that may be left behind the drags with their sacks and slickers. Sometimes the riders haul the drags in opposite directions, depending upon the direction in which the fire is traveling. The riders who are handling the drags ride on a trot in order to put the fire out as quickly as possible.

Back firing is a device often resorted to to check an approaching fire. The idea is to burn over a strip about thirty to forty feet wide to serve as a fire guard. With a burning sack or a bunch of flaming weeds a man goes along setting fire to the grass while the other fire fighters stand watch and whip the blaze out when it has gone far enough. When the approaching fire reaches the burned-over fire guard, it will die out; but the fire fighters will have to watch out and see to it that the flames do not leap over the guard barrier. This often happens if a strong wind is blowing. Blazing embers of grass and dry cow chips are generally blown for some distance and if they are not put out, they are apt to set another fire to charging across the country.

THE BILL OF RIGHTS

The Bill of Rights: A Transcription
    The Preamble to The Bill of Rights
    Congress of the United States begun and held at the City of New York, on Wednesday the fourth of March, one thousand seven hundred and eighty nine.

The Conventions of a number of the States, having at the time of their adopting the Constitution, expressed a desire, in order to prevent misconstruction or abuse of its powers, that further declaratory and restrictive clauses should be added: And as extending the ground of public confidence in the Government, will best ensure the beneficent ends of its institution.

Resolved by the Senate and House of Representatives of the United States of America, in Congress assembled, two thirds of both Houses concurring, that the following Articles be proposed to the Legislatures of the several States, as amendments to the Constitution of the United States, all, or any of which Articles, when ratified by three fourths of the said Legislatures, to be valid to all intents and purposes, as part of the said Constitution; viz. Articles in addition to, and Amendment of the Constitution of the United States of America, proposed by Congress, and ratified by the Legislatures of the several States, pursuant to the fifth Article of the original Constitution.

Amendment I

Congress shall make no law respecting an establishment of religion, or prohibiting the free exercise thereof; or abridging the freedom of speech, or of the press; or the right of the people peaceably to assemble, and to petition the Government for a redress of grievances.

Amendment II

A well regulated Militia, being necessary to the security of a free State, the right of the people to keep and bear Arms, shall not be infringed.

Amendment III

No Soldier shall, in time of peace, be quartered in any house, without the consent of the Owner, nor in time of war, but in a manner to be prescribed by law.

Amendment IV

The right of the people to be secure in their persons, houses, papers, and effects, against unreasonable searches and seizures, shall not be violated, and no Warrants shall issue, but upon probable cause, supported by Oath or affirmation, and particularly describing the place to be searched, and the persons or things to be seized.

Amendment V

No person shall be held to answer for a capital, or otherwise infamous crime, unless on a presentment or indictment of a Grand Jury, except in cases arising in the land or naval forces, or in the Militia, when in actual service in time of War or public danger; nor shall any person be subject for the same offence to be twice put in jeopardy of life or limb; nor shall be compelled in any criminal case to be a witness against himself, nor be deprived of life, liberty, or property, without due process of law; nor shall private property be taken for public use, without just compensation.

Amendment VI

In all criminal prosecutions, the accused shall enjoy the right to a speedy and public trial, by an impartial jury of the State and district wherein the crime shall have been committed, which district shall have been previously ascertained by law, and to be informed of the nature and cause of the accusation; to be confronted with the witnesses against him; to have compulsory process for obtaining witnesses in his favor, and to have the Assistance of Counsel for his defence.

Amendment VII

In Suits at common law, where the value in controversy shall exceed twenty dollars, the right of trial by jury shall be preserved, and no fact tried by a jury, shall be otherwise re-examined in any Court of the United States, than according to the rules of the common law.

Amendment VIII

Excessive bail shall not be required, nor excessive fines imposed, nor cruel and unusual punishments inflicted.

Amendment IX

The enumeration in the Constitution, of certain rights, shall not be construed to deny or disparage others retained by the people.

Amendment X

The powers not delegated to the United States by the Constitution, nor prohibited by it to the States, are reserved to the States respectively, or to the people.

SAGAS EVERY BOY SHOULD READ

MULTI VOLUME

The *Harry Potter* series by J. K. Rowling
A History of the English-Speaking Peoples by Winston S. Churchill
The *Hornblower* series by C. S. Forester
The Leather-Stocking Tales by James Fenimore Cooper

The Lord of the Rings (trilogy) by J. R. R. Tolkien
The Narnia series by C. S. Lewis
The Redwall series by Brian Jacques

SINGLE VOLUME AND SHORT STORY

The Autobiography of Malcolm X
The Adventures of Huckleberry Finn by Mark Twain
The Adventures of Robin Hood by Howard Pyle
The Adventures of Sherlock Holmes by Arthur Connan Doyle
The Adventures of Tom Sawyer by Mark Twain
Around the World in Eighty Days by Jules Verne
The Bear by William Faulkner
The Iliad by Homer
Johnny Tremain by Ester Forbes
Kidnapped by Robert Louis Stevenson
The Kite Runner by Khaled Hosseini
Leiningen Versus the Ants by Carl Stephenson
The Light in the Forest by Conrad Richter
Lord Jim by Joseph Conrad
Lord of the Flies by William Golding
Moby Dick by Herman Melville
The Odyssey by Homer
The Prince and the Pauper by Mark Twain
The Prisoner of Zenda by Anthony Hope
The Red Badge of Courage by Stephen Crane
A Tale of Two Cities by Charles Dickens
Tarzan of the Apes by Edgar Rice Burroughs
Treasure Island by Robert Louis Stevenson
The Three Musketeers by Alexandre Dumas
Young Men and Fire by Norman Maclean
Youth by Joseph Conrad
Zen in the Art of Archery by Eugen Herrigel

APPENDIX

BOY'S CLUBS AND ORGANIZATIONS

Boys and Girls Club of America
http://www.bgca.org/

Boy Scouts of America National Council
http://www.scouting.org/nav/enter.jsp?s=mc

National Rifle Association Youth Programs
http://www.nrahq.org/youth/index.asp

Police Athletic League
http://www.palnyc.org

Future Farmers of America
http://www.ffa.org/

Rotary International
http://www.rotary.org/

The Audubon Society
http://www.audubon.org/educate/index.php

4-H
http://www.4husa.org/

Sierra Club
http://www.sierraclub.org/youth/

Fishing Works Youth Club Directory
http://www.fishingworks.com/youth-clubs/

USA Archery Junior Olympic Archery Development
http://www.usarchery.org/html/JOAD.html

Outward Bound Wilderness Youth
http://outwardboundwilderness.org/age/youth.html

Kid's Gardening
http://www.kidsgardening.com/

U.S. Junior Orienteering
http://www.us.orienteering.org/

U.S. Sailing – Youth Sailing
http://www.ussailing.org/youth/

National Park Service – Archaeology for Kids
http://www.nps.gov/archeology/public/kids/index.htm

American Red Cross – Youth Services
http://www.redcross.org/services/youth/0,1082,0_326_,00.html

United States Lifesaving Association – Junior Lifeguards
http://www.usla.org/LGtoLG/junior.asp

Shooting and Youth Organizations
http://www.remington.com/about/conservation.asp

Bassmaster Youth Programs
http://sports.espn.go.com/outdoors/bassmaster/youth/news/
story?page=b_youth_program_overview

USA Karate
http://www.usakarate.org/

USA Jiu Jitsu Federation
http://www.wkf.org/jj.html

U.S. Fencing Youth Development
http://www.usfaryc.org/Welcome.html

U.S.A. Climbing
http://www.usaclimbing.net/home.cfm

Indoor Climbing Walls Directory
http://www.indoorclimbing.com/

Directory of Local Outdoors Programs –
http://www.youthoutdoorslegacyfund.com/funds.html

NOTES

NOTES

NOTES

NOTES

NOTES

NOTES

NOTES

NOTES

NOTES

NOTES

NOTES

NOTES